The MLM Junkie Success Formula by Mervyn Chan

7 Proven Strategies to Building a Network Marketing Empire in 12 months

Mervyn Chan

DISCLAIMER:

This book details the author's personal experiences with and opinions about network marketing. The author is not licensed as an educational consultant, teacher, psychologist, or psychiatrist.

The author and publisher are providing this book and its contents on an "as is" basis and make no representations or warranties of any kind with respect to this book or its contents. The author and publisher disclaim all such representations and warranties, including for example warranties of merchantability and educational or medical advice for a particular purpose. In addition, the author and publisher do not represent or warrant that the information accessible via this book is accurate, complete or current.

The statements made about products and services have not been evaluated by the Singapore government. Please consult with your own legal or accounting professional regarding the suggestions and recommendations made in this book.

Except as specifically stated in this book, neither the author or publisher, nor any authors, contributors, or other representatives will be liable for damages arising out of or in connection with the use of this book. This is a comprehensive limitation of liability that applies to all damages of any kind, including (without limitation) compensatory; direct, indirect or consequential damages; loss of data, income or profit; loss of or damage to property and claims of third parties.

You understand that this book is not intended as a substitute for consultation with a licensed medical, educational, legal or accounting professional. Before you begin any change in your lifestyle in any way, you will consult a licensed professional to ensure that you are doing what's best for your situation.

This book provides content related to educational, medical, and psychological topics. As such, use of this book implies your acceptance of this disclaimer.

Copyright © 2016 Mervyn Chan

All rights reserved.

ISBN:
978-981-11-1233-1

DEDICATION

To my gorgeous mom, dad, mentors, coaches, team mates and to the dreamers. Without you, this business wouldn't exist.

CONTENTS

	Acknowledgments	i
1	Myths and Truths	7
2	Why I do MLM	25
3	Traditional MLM methods	36
4	MLM the New Age Way	48
5	How to Choose a MLM	59
6	Compensation Plan	69
7	Vision for Lifestyle and Leadership	91
8	Why people fail?	103
9	"Pipeline" Pablo and Bruno Story	122
10	7 Proven Strategies to Building a Network Marketing Empire in 12 Months	131

ACKNOWLEDGMENTS

I would like to express my appreciation to Jeffery Tan and team who helped with proofreading drafts and publication. I am most grateful for their assistance, which helped with the process immensely. They have made this a much more powerful resource for you.

Introduction

For more than 10 years, I have been exploring different platforms to be successful. I have been top sales person and top producer for several different companies from IT tech to digital marketing agency to seminar business.

This year, I decided to venture 'full force' into MLM business and amazingly, I created a 5 figure passive income stream in less than 8 weeks and has organizations all around the world including Colombia, Panama, Costa Rica, Chile, Peru, Brunei, Malaysia and of course Singapore.

MLM is getting more and more popular these days. By far, historically and statistically, MLM industry has created the most millionaires.

My experience in MLM was not like 10 or 20 years. In fact I still remember the first MLM company which I joined was in 2014, on a part time basis and with a 'try' mentality. It is a USA company and I was sold the idea of being a pioneer in Singapore. Without full support from the USA side because of distance and I had to figure out things on myself, the team quiet down.

With several trial and errors after joining a few companies, of course spending some money to buy products as well, in 2016, I managed to create a 5 figure passive income stream in less than 8 weeks. And I helped many other people do the same. A few are staying home mothers. On a recent incentive trip to USA, after conversations with other MLM leaders, I can proudly say that the results that me and my team created are much faster than most of them.

This book is organized because I want to help more newbies out there to be able to make a sound decision for themselves whether MLM is for them and how to choose which MLM company to join. I still can remember when I first started; I do not have a proper coach or mentor to guide me. Every leader claim that they are the best and joining them is the right decision or choice. I had a lot of lost time which I can't make back now. I certainly feel that these lost time could have be saved should there someone to coach or mentor or guide me.

Yours sincerely,

Mervyn Chan

1. MYTHS AND TRUTHS

Historically, sales staff has been forced to grind for hours daily to meet quotas. Those playing the numbers game often struggled to make ends meet. A commission based sales job puts you at the complete mercy of your customer base, and the industry in general. As new products come out, old ones become obsolete and so on. This can make it difficult to keep up when trying to handle everything alone. Multi Level Marketing companies, or Network Marketing, as they are commonly referred to, are the wave of the future.

It is 2016, and technology is booming more so than any previous era. There is an abundance of new fangled ways to do things, and old sales traditions are dying hard. Today, we have to consider things like, why use paper promotions when we have digital technology that can spread the word in seconds? Save time, save money, right? Why use snail mail when we can help the environment by sending an email promotion, not to mention save a tree? Best of all, why should one sales person work extended hours trying to do everything alone, when they can utilize the benefits of an MLM structure? A good sales rep will thrive in this type of environment, especially with all access advertising at the touch of a button. The MLM is at the top of the food chain when it comes to digital marketing advantages.

As with all new ideas that can quickly rise to the top, there are myths and truths of MLM and network marketing that raise questions. These concerns cause some traditional sales people to shy away from the modern marketing strategy. There really is no reason to find fault with a successful strategy, but MLMs meet with a great deal of scrutiny. This is primarily due to opinions in the industry based on stereotypical myths. It is unfortunate that some people automatically assume the myths are true, instead of delving a little deeper to get to the truth. MLMs aren't trying to hide anything. All you have to do in order to see the true benefits is look a little deeper.

So, what are the myths and truths of MLM and network marketing that is coming on like a tornado through Kansas, leaving the sales tactics of the past in its dust? Let us take a look at the 3 common myths, and the 3 most common truths mentioned in the industry.

1. Myths and Truths

Myths # 1: MLM is get rich quick scheme.

There are those that yearn to find the perfect get rich scheme for many reasons. People fall on hard times, acquire unexpected financial woes, and accidents do happen. In cases like that, quick cash can be a true blessing. With that said, sorry, the rumour that MLM is a get rich scheme is most assuredly a myth.

A Multi Level Marketing company may seem like a get rich quick scam due to the enthusiasm of those who are successful. It may seem too good to be true, but it isn't. The confusion comes from lack of understanding of how the system works. Many naysayers out on the message boards will complain of investing and not getting a return, but they do not talk about actually "working" to achieve a return on the investments. In most cases, it is like they join the MLM under the expectation that money will simply be handed to them while they sit back and patiently wait. That is not the case.

An MLM, just like any other type of company, takes work and effort. You cannot just join multi level marketing organizations and not do any type of marketing. That attitude in general is likely how the myth got started. As with any business, you DO have to put in efforts in order to see the fruits of those labours. The more you do, the more you make. The less you do, the less your attempts will flourish and profit. You cannot enter an MLM with the simple expectation that you will get paid regardless. Most successful business opportunities did not become successful by giving away free money to people that do nothing to earn it.

The positive aspect to putting in hard work with this type of company is that you will see benefits from your labours. Unlike get rich quick schemes, working with an MLM allows for actual payments which will come in. You won't consistently hear excuses as to how many more weeks till payday. Everyone profits from the sales, not just the top tier executives. There is no, "it will take some extra time to get paid," situations in a real multi level marketing company. Things are constantly moving, growing and evolving to the next levels.

Myths #2: MLM is a scam.

We have to be realistic. Every year, there are millions of businesses started that end up being a scam, but "real" Multi Level Marketing companies are not, in most cases. Occasionally you might run into an MLM that is a scam, but the difference is, it was never a real MLM to begin with. Most companies like that actually start out with the intention of scamming individuals, or employees. It is also possible those who initiated the business got greedy, and the company evolved into a scam. One could go to work in an office that withholds pay for the first pay period, meaning a potential wait of 3 to 4 weeks for the first paycheck. When pay day comes, the office might be empty and the company gone. An employer might get audited by the IRAS (Inland Revenue Authority of Singapore. For readers in United States of America or other countries, it may be known as IRS). When this happens, all the assets can quickly become frozen depending on the circumstances, such as tax delinquency. Worst case scenarios in situations such as those, the employee often doesn't learn of the problem until overdraft charges occur in their own accounts. Things like this have happened since the dawn of employer, employee relations.

The important takeaway on that note is that ANY company can be a scam. It is up to the employee or contractor to confirm the legitimacy of that business. This is the digital era. In many cases, everything we need to know is at the touch of a button, or a phone call away. In Singapore, The Consumers Association of Singapore (CASE) is a non-profit, non-governmental organisation that is committed towards protecting consumers interest through information and education, and promoting an environment of fair and ethical trade practices. One of our key achievements is in advocating for the Consumer Protection (Fair Trading) Act (CPFTA) which came into effect on March 1, 2004. Or you can utilize resources like the Better Business Bureau, which is a nonprofit organization that takes complaints and positive input on companies all across the United States. You can also look for information online in regards to the length of time the company has been in business, the structure of the business, and the executives that represent the face of the company. Google might be your best friend when trying to figure out the legitimacy of a perspective employer… or potential scam artist.

Myths #3: MLM is pyramid scheme.

It is not difficult to understand how a multi level marketing company can be perceived as a network of pyramid schemes. The very structure of the business is a pyramid, but realistically, that is the structure of any business if you look at a diagram. There will always be those on the top. In corporate situations, this is the Board of Directors, Presidents, and Vice Presidents of the corporation. Most of those guys consider the board meeting their work. In smaller businesses, you might just have the owner, a manager, assistant manager, or shift supervisor. Even in the contracting world, there are lead workers that ensure all other workers know and do what is required in order to fulfil the contract. That lead person usually deals with the contract holder as well. There will always be some type of business structure which resembles a pyramid. The amount of people involved decreases closer to the top, but that does not make multi level marketing companies a pyramid scam.

The standard business structure in America and Singapore is that those in control make the most. From there, the money trickles down to the entry level employees with everyone making various amounts according to position. In a pyramid scheme, those entry level people seldom ever see any benefits, including pay. When it comes to an MLM, everyone benefits from product sales, from the founder to the newest member of the company. This is no different than any other legitimate company in the country, other than it is based on sales and commissions.

A commission based job is also a red flag for a pyramid scheme, but no so in the case of an MLM. Being based on commissions both adds potential to the earnings, and can make life a little unpredictable. A commission based job in most cases has no guarantees, like that of a broker or a used car salesman. Multi level media companies are different in the fact they have products that have been proven successful. If the product and the company check out, than most likely the commissions will be checking out above the standard as well. Don't fear the MLM.

Still not convinced? With or without you, the evolution still goes on. That is the beauty of our modern, digital age. You can find out what you want too. You can do as much or as little research as you like involving the company you suspect of being a pyramid scheme. No reliable multi level marketing company will care if someone investigates them to ensure the stability of the business. No legitimate business cares, unless they have something to hide. There are several things to do in order to increase one's confidence in an MLM opportunity.

How long has the company been in business? A pyramid scam will normally achieve a big score of three, and then close its doors. Many times they do this to clear the air and reopen later under a new name. A quality MLM will be in business for a while. They might be a startup, but they will have an established paper trail showing consistency and allowing for recognition of their own unique form of branding. An MLM will be proud, confident, and not ashamed to show the community, nor the world, that they exist and plan to evolve and thrive with time.

What type of compensations and fees are involved? In many cases, a pyramid scheme will try to get a new employee to purchase a package or starter kit. This can be a very tricky situation, so be prepared to ask questions. If the recruiter starts to get flustered and evades answering queries, you might want to re-evaluate the potential job offer. If they become more aggressive in their tactics as more inquiries are made… definitely hold off on investing until an opportunity to really do some research is possible.

Be specific when it comes to compensation before agreeing to any contracts. Scammers will usually give very vague details when it comes to what an entry level position will make. They push for the lower tier hires to put in more work and focus on getting promoted because, "that is where the real money is." The sad reality is that in many cases the companies that evade compensation questions or give unrealistic answers are usually a pyramid or a corrupt organization.

Multi level marketing companies make their money on the actual sales, not new member contributions. They want good sales people and are willing to compensate and provide legitimate calculations for potential new staff associates. Applicants will get realistic figures when they ask for them. The company should have a website, paperwork, or some concrete information so that they can provide potential earning details. This should never be a subject that a legitimate company hesitates with.

You can often discover the truth of a pyramid scheme company by requesting concrete data in regards to entry level sales staff profit margins, monthly and annually. You want to be specific, as the executive sales figures will not be beneficial. Ask not only for potential earnings, but for the when, where and what style of transfer the funds one can expect. The recruiter will often become evasive, changing the subject. Sometimes they will hand over a print out with some ridiculous figures on it that don't make sense, while talking you in circles about going for a higher position. Overall, you will likely leave without ever getting a legitimate answer to the question involving pay.

Do online research on not only the company, but the executives in the company. Use keywords like pyramid scam, pyramid schemes, scam, reputation, and review. You might find a few good reviews, as real pyramid schemes have been known to pay people to write faux reviews in their favor. You can also check for positive reviews, and look for uniform writing and key word phrases such as, "made me rich" and "get rich quick". The Better Business Bureau is a quality search tool to utilize if trying to determine if a company is legitimate if you are unsure where to look.

Check out the company product, especially the refund policy. If a company has a reliable product, there will be reviews. Some pyramid structures make their profits by selling underlings low quality products. When the new staff member cannot sell the product, a pyramid scam might not give a refund, and in most cases if they do, it is only a small percentage of the original cost. The product is very important, so pay close attention to exactly what it is, what it is made of, what it does, and all warranty information and clauses. The clause can be the catch.

Now, let us move on to the truths about multi level marketing companies, which you might find surprising.

Truth #1: An MLM requires work.

Some people join an MLM under the assumption they can sit back and watch the money flow in. They imagine themselves sitting at home and getting richer by the month thanks to the hard work and such of other people. Their job is to watch over these profits and ensure that other people "beneath" them are actually doing what they are supposed to and pumping out the product or service the company is known for in the industry. If one goes into a multi level marketing company with the attitude no real work is involved, they will be sadly mistaken. The income received with no work will also likely be very disappointing.

Any successful business takes work, and plenty of it. It doesn't necessarily have to be difficult work, but it is work none the less. If it is sales, one has to commit to putting effort into your product. If it is services, one has to push those services in the areas that they will be most beneficial. Whatever the position, it will take effort in order to achieve the success. The more a sales person puts into their marketing plan, the better things will be.

The marketing plan is potentially the most important part of a sales person's job. You look at the product, evaluate it, and meditate on its uses, including pros and cons. A good rep knows every aspect of the product they are trying to promote. Once the product is known, it is time to create the perfect marketing plan on how to promote it. Use every tool at your disposal, from friends, to businesses to digital tools. The marketing strategy is the business plan of sales, and will be the success or failure the venture. Some sales people have worked for years to create the perfect plan to sell whatever product required.

Truth #2: An MLM is a form of marketing.

This is an absolute truth. The thought that one can conduct any type of business without utilizing a marketing plan of some type is not realistic. Every product and service out there requires some sort of tactic to get the word out and gain the interest of the targeted audience. An MLM is ideal, because you have multiple people with multiple different strengths and skill sets, all working together for the good of multi level marketing. The answer to that statement falls in the very name… MLM.

An MLM is a sales oriented company. Profits are made not only by one's own sales, but by ALL sales. This means everyone needs to be motivated to sale by any moral means necessary. It is of the utmost importance that we take advantage of each and every possibility within our reach. The most powerful tool that can be utilized in today's modern marketing strategy is social media.

The digital age has opened so many doors that it is near impossible not to find a reliable outlet for marketing with ease. We have a variety of social media outlets that literally travel with us everywhere. We have professional social media platforms, like LinkedIn. It is a fantastic site for the professional profile and introduction to the MLM representative. The majority of the users on this platform are professional individuals in one field or another. LinkedIn can be a great way to initiate contacts to share information and potential deals with. It can be utilized to post new plans, products and services that might cater to other professional individuals, or potentially one of their own clients.

Next, we have social media profiles like Facebook, Tumblr, and Google+. Each of these can be utilized as a small profile. They allow a short introduction to the MLM, but also allow endless information sharing potential. These sites can be utilized as a way to promote new products or services easily. Social media like this allows us to virtually communicate with perspective clients and increase of consumer base in all industries. Facebook is the most widely used social media platform out there, with millions of individual and business profiles. People share everything from pictures of their children and animals, to what they had for breakfast. It is a marketer's dream platform. Every iota of potentially useful information is available to us, because the consumers provide it.

Another wonder of the digital age for MLM companies are the quick information sites. Twitter and Instagram, are quick social sharing sites. Each is great when it comes to a short statements, link marketing, or social networking to get the name or product out. You follow and gain followers. Those people see whatever information you happen to tweet about. Instagram allows you to post an image with a caption and hashtags. Both of these outlets are fantastic when it comes to promotion. Some professionals are shocked by the increased potential that can come with these simple platforms.

Each social media platform allows one to increase the potential for sales. The important thing is to home those inner communication skills towards the social media sites. Not everyone is successful when it comes to social media. Some completely flop and come across as pushy or to nerdy. Check out similar tweets and posts on the social channels to see how other MLMs are taking advantage of the new marketing technology. There is no shame in exploration. Those who have the largest followers or friends lists are doing something right. The more people signed on to view, the more views. An increase in views can be an increase in sales.

What type of format are these successful social media MLMs using? Do not duplicate, but embrace inspiration and run forward. Improve your own social media profile by keeping information up to date. It is also very important to maintain a social presence. Do not set up a page and let it set for days on in with little or no activity. The more people see your posts and tweets, the more they will know you exist. There is a fine line between reminding people you exist, and annoying people with your existence. A good MLM marketer knows the difference, and walks that line well.

Social media is not limited to platforms like Facebook. There are message boards, groups specializing in everything imaginable, and sites designated for discussions about different products and services. These groups and different venues allow us to post from different perspectives, sometimes casually suggesting a product, or giving an opinion on one. Joining these types of online communities allows the consumers to see us as human beings and not aggressive sale people. Technique is important in sales.

It has been proven that the better one is at utilizing social media tools, the more successful the business can be. When it comes to any sales or service, this is true. This is especially true when in an MLM company. Sales involves socializing and the modern version is all about social media. If you utilize the available platforms correctly the product you promote will not only be on your page, it will travel across the country to everyone who can get online.

Mobile platforms are all the rage in today's market. Creating a mobile app via social media can triple the amount of sales. This means your product is not only popular online for that utilizing computers and laptops, but it is also being used on all mobile devices. This includes phones, tablets, the Google Glass and the new mobile communication watch. A smart MLM representative will take advantage of the mobile world.

Truth #3: An MLM is not your company; you are working with or for the company.

When it comes to multi level marketing companies, the individual never really owns the company. That is not a bad, it is just realistic. No matter the position, or how long you work with an MLM, marketing is consistent work. You have to put in efforts in order to reap benefits. The journey starts with the product and ends with the product. The entire process in an MLM is based on what is being sold and the representative's ability to spread the word and get it out there. Tradition has taught us that the sales people that get out and pound the pavement are the ones that really benefit in the industry. Thanks to the coming of the digital age, that is no longer the way things work. Hitting the road and doing personal sales can still be beneficial, but it is not as necessary as it was a few decades ago.

In a way, the product owns the company and the representative. A quality product will get sales and garner a reputation just as quickly as a bad one. Once the product is known, the job of the representative becomes a lot easier.

One simply has to continue promoting sales via social media tools, and any other means that are both moral, and potentially lucrative. Eventually, after getting up a strong client base and continuing to put a little time in for new ones, a good MLM representative can achieve those dreams of putting in a little "less" physical work.

We have so many options at our disposable to utilize for marketing purposes; there is no limit to what we can accomplish. The important aspect of sales is that we promote and sell a quality product. Once you have sold people something faulty and cheap, they don't often forget. At the same time, if you happen to have sold them a fantastic appliance that is still a part of their day to day routine 3 years later, they will have trust. When they see that name or face in the future, it will be related to the cheaply made product, or that fantastic product you sold them in the past.

The future of marketing is the multi level marketing groups. Why deal with 5 different companies to promote your product or service when a one stop shop can take care of every need involved in the marketing process. MLMs often have a dedicated group of sales specialists that have both experience, and unique, well evaluated marketing plans. The sales staff will be just as motivated to sell the product as the creator. Why? Because that is how they make the money. That is how the entire structure makes money. The more that is sold, the more lucrative for everyone involved.

There are many myths and truths of MLM and network marketing out there. It just takes a little common sense and research to sort out the quality companies from those that are pyramid or get rich quick schemes. With so many tools at our disposal, getting to the truth is no longer a challenge. The topics covered in this chapter are the primary concerns that seem to surround MLM companies, and cause some quality sales people to avoid them like a plague. If those individuals took the time to evaluate the potential job, they might find it to be a way to accomplish any dreams in their future.

Paid for incentive trip to Bahamas Atlantis Paradise Island

Notes

2. WHY I DO MLM

When people ask about my career, they often appear shocked when I proudly say network marketing and MLM. Why? They automatically assume MLM means pyramid scheme, and are surprised I'd be involved in such a thing. Understanding the stereotypical image that follows MLMs like a dark shadow, it is my pleasure to surprise those with curiosities, and shed some light to make that shadow disappear.

It is easy to exude professional confidence when one is a part of a legitimate MLM company. There is a deep inner satisfaction when one can perform network marketing on the highest professional level, and shatter stereotypes. Promoting quality products with quality people and sharing in the overall success of those companies and individuals is a way of being successful while giving back.

Why get involved and continue to run a successful MLM? Despite the negative publicity and stereotypical labelling that comes with network marketing companies, not all of them are bad. This one falls in the, "isn't bad" category. Not only is it highly legitimate with high quality products and customer service, we maintain a level of excellence that stands out in a crowd. You will never see someone pointing at me and saying, "that guy, he sold me something terrible." In fact, it is more likely you might see the opposite reaction. MLM has helped me go from your average Joe, to a successful person who can be proud of what gets done daily. I am a man whose children can hold their heads high knowing I worked hard to get where I am, and will continue to do so.

Just because you make it to the top doesn't mean you stop. You have to keep on going, setting goals, and making improvements. The only real limitations we have in life are the ones we set for ourselves. I choose to ignore limitations and continue setting goals, becoming all that is possible during this lifetime. I hope it emanates the image that hard work can continue to pay off. It is when you quit trying that success can grow stagnant.

1. Dreams and Goals.

It all starts with a dream. In our youth most of us strive to do something with our lives. It might be something simple, like owning a farm and living off the land. It could be starting an MLM and creating a successful company filled with like minded individuals who devote their time and energy into finding and promoting quality products or services. It could be both. It could be more. Dreams are whatever we want them to be. My dream was to find an honest way to become successful and continue helping people in some way.

As we get older, we begin to set goals with the hope that they will be achieved, and quickly make our dreams come true. Of course, quickly is just a dream in itself in most cases. Setting small goals and achieving them will slowly help to not only build confidence, but also build relationships. These relationships continue to grow and evolve, as do our goals. As the cycle continues, you get to a point where you wake up smiling, as you realize… dreams really can come true.

2. My experience as an employee

When you see me, you might not be able to imagine the not so confident individual that once existed in this body. Dealing with mundane jobs, financial discomfort, and knowing I was missing out on life. I had set aside my goals and put my dreams on hold for jobs that just weren't going anywhere.

You may not believe this, but I've experienced firsthand the inconveniences that can occur when the boss delays salary. The CPF (The Central Provident Fund is a social security savings plan for citizens old age. Employers are required to contribute 17% of the salary amount for employees below age 55) doesn't get paid, the bills get behind, no gas in the car, cupboards get bare, and when you finally do get a check, that money is already spent. You pay the bills, get some groceries and gas, than that check is gone and the cycle starts again. That is not living… it is just going through the motions of surviving.

As an employee, we have no control over time, ours, nor that of what is going on around us. We have no control over what we have to accomplish during the day. Our goals are the employer's goals in order to keep those checks rolling in. There comes a point when you have to say, enough is enough. I want the power back over my own life. I want to set my own goals and make the dreams I put on hold come true. It is like waking up and taking the reins back on life.

3. Owning a traditional business is a great start

Starting a business is a great way to retake control, but there is a lot of responsibility that comes with owning a company, especially the traditional type. You have to pay rental for an office space on top of your home. Either do your own accounting or hire a professional, and pay employees. Depending on the number of employees, an accountant can be a necessity, than you pay the employees, the bills in both places, and the accountant to write all the checks. The business begins to thrive but it can take over your life.

Once again, you feel yourself start to slip away under the weight of the rigid, traditional business structure. An inner voice is screaming, "I'm suffocating!" It is like a re-awakening, or a self evolution, except this one stirs up memories of those original dreams. A business that is more free flowing and not as obstinate in its rules. One that allows a person to move at their own pace, doing as much or as little as you want, and surviving with those choices, because you made them.

4. Personal Development

What is it about doing MLM that helps us in life as individuals and encourages personal development? One of the main factors about doing an MLM, is that it helps me with my own self evolution. MLM helps build my confidence, along with an abundance of interpersonal skills with other fellow human beings. Initiating an MLM was a time of inner development, self evaluation, and change. The beginning of this organization was a time of digging deep inside, and really focusing on what I wanted, and needed in order to make life liveable in a more positive, less restrictive way. I gained confidence, and educated myself further on the things it would take to evoke true happiness.

Once I realized who I really was inside, it was like becoming a butterfly, spreading my wings, setting the right goals, and interacting with like minded individuals. The MLM structure is 100% people oriented, so even the most antisocial individual most learn to interact and embrace other individuals. The MLM aided me on learning to really work with others on a deep, professional level. I developed a better understanding of those around me, and it was like an awakening.

It is amazing the difference it can make in one's life when you really start to understand how to work with others. Anyone can punch a time clock, but with an MLM, time clocks don't exist. Instead, we band together in the collective spirit as a team.

This strengthened me in a multitude of ways. It increased my own inner confidence, which allowed me to spread that confidence out to my team. The MLM allowed me to increase my communication skills. This strengthened my ability to communicate with my team, and more easily represent the ideas that I was formulating in my own mind.

Overall, the MLM helped me improve as a person, improving areas I once felt weak in, and making the aspects of my inner self that were on the right path even better. Becoming involved in an MLM literally helped create the man who now writes this book, and I encourage others to consider the possibilities and potential within themselves like I did. It can be a truly life altering experience. It has been for me.

5. Recognition

Once we evolve into the metaphorical butterfly and start setting goals, we hope for recognition with these efforts. For instance, if the field is sales, such as with an MLM, it takes working hard and keeping yourself on top. No quality efforts will go unrecognized if you are in the right field, and doing what you are meant to do.

We all go through periods of adjustment, trying to find the place we best fit in. Some individuals are just naturals, but others have to struggle to find their place in life.

Other than getting recognize on stage with award presentation or incentive trips, we also have to "recognize" where we belong, but we must work to achieve our place. Once we have that confidence in ourselves, and feel secure in the products we have chose to promote, others will recognize that confidence as well. Once they do, you might find yourself surprised by how quickly things can escalate. Before you know it, you will be living the dream. In doing so and not giving up, you can help others to recognize their own potential.

6. Building a team.

This is the interesting and challenging stage. Once the metamorphosis is complete in our own lives, it is time to move forward and continue to build upwards. We have found products that are the key to the door of success, and it is time to spread the word in the MLM industry. The best way to do this is to bring others into the fold.

This can be a tedious process at first. We are fighting against the stereotypical comparisons between network marketing and pyramid schemes, and the reputation is scandalous. This can cause a few bumps in the road when trying to find like minded individuals who want to work hard, set goals and follow their dreams too.

Why do most people avoid bumps? One reason is simply fear. Many individuals are actually afraid to step out of the 9 to 5 box and branch out on a commission based job. They are scared that they won't be able to make ends meet, that they'll have to work harder to do so, or that the MLM is actually a scam. Though a legitimate MLM is not a pyramid scheme, qualified people will shy away because of the similarities. This is unfortunate, as fear might keep them in the box forever.

Another potential bump comes due to the similarity between a legitimate MLM and a pyramid scheme, those that feed on the pyramids might approach you as well. They might bring faulty products and have deceptive motives. These are not the individuals we want to add to a budding team of hard working, dream followers. If they are shady, ruthless and don't have confidence in the products and services in this MLM, they are not the kind of team players needed. The wrong type of sales person on a team can make successful dreams come tumbling down.

Above all, a good MLM team is a positive group of individuals who are willing to set goals, and keep working hard in order to fulfil those goals. Qualified team players will have dreams of their own and they will want to succeed. Greater success comes with teamwork, which requires team players. This means we all need to be on the same page with products and services. All team members do not require the same skill set. As a matter of fact, versatility within a team is a beautiful thing and creates a balanced group. Some might have strengths with direct communication; others might be gods in the social networking realm. Digital technology aids in all areas. A good team creates a stronger heartbeat for the MLM.

It isn't always easy finding a success in our own lives, but it can be done. We might have to climb metaphorical mountains and jump through metaphorical hoops for a while, but we can create the life we want if the desire is strong enough. There are no caps on an MLM and network marketing. We can make as much as we want, as long as the desire and determination is there to work for it. In my opinion, making one's dreams come true is well worth the efforts.

Internet Marketing Workshop

Notes

3. TRADITIONAL MLM METHODS

After the realization that multi level marketing is not in any way a pyramid scheme, I gained a huge interest in the untapped potential at my fingertips. Now was the time to move forward, not tomorrow, or next week. I was swept up in the limitless opportunities to help both myself and others. Not only could I make an incredible amount of money and support my family, but I could also provide a service to my clients by providing them with something they need.

The first step was figuring out the steps necessary to create a successful business opportunity in the MLM industry. After doing a little research, it was very easy to see that there were already a collection of proven methods available. All I had to do was invest my time and energy into taking the first step.

1. ABC.

Many or most people start off their MLM or Network Marketing business by prospecting their friends and family.

These people, no doubt trust you the most, but they are also the hardest prospect you will get. Without proper handling of your appointment with them, you can forget about recruiting them to your network.

This is because friends tend to be more judgmental of you, and they view you as an equal, therefore it is not easy opening them up to listen to you. During the presentation, some may joke, and are not serious in the presentation, some may also give you objections before you start your presentation.

Therefore, as a new comer to the industry, it is good to have your upline who is willing to help you in your first few appointments with your friends. They are the best people to leverage upon. You need to practice the rule of ABC during presentations when your upline is helping you.

ABC

A- Advisor (your upline)
B- B- Bridge (you)
C- C- Customer (your prospect/ friend)

It's your job to bridge the gap between your friend and your upline. Give background about your friend to your upline, and let your friend know why you respect this upline so much. During the presentation, you should sit by your friend, giving support throughout the presentation.

You should always be around during such presentation to show respect to your upline and friend. Try not to give advice and "try to help" your upline, during the presentation, this will undermine your upline's authority.

Just sit there and agree to what he says is the best help you can give. You will be the one closing your friend to join you in the business, not your upline. Give moral support to your friend and assure him that joining you will be the right choice.

You should also be doing problem solving if your friend is reluctant or indecisive. Give support as a friend, so you won't be too aggressive or pushy. It's not worth losing a friend over this.

There are no real secrets in the MLM industry using traditional methods. Motivated individuals have to dive right in and take the bull by the horns.

The first thing to do is to prepare and start building a team. An upline advisor can show the potential team the good reasons required to get the ball rolling. Your job is to paint a portrait of success in the traditional MLM network marketing business opportunities.

The majority of people in an MLM initiate a team by bringing in family and friends. These are the people in our lives that trust us the most, but can also provide the most scrutiny.

They may not take you seriously, or they may joke around and make light of the network marketing industry. It is of the utmost importance that the presentation is flawless, thus having someone from the upline to accompany and aid in these initial presentations can be a life saver.

We bridge the gap between our friends and our upline in order to build a happy team with a healthy, motivated environment. We bridge the gap between our friends and the upline by letting the upline know important information about our friends.

This allows the advisor to make a positive presentation based on the individual, not on a stranger. We should avoid jumping in unless it is to help the upline, as you never want to upstage or undermine during a presentation.

Try to sit, agree, nod and encourage your friends or family members to listen and understand.

The customer or prospect, aka your friend or family member, you don't want to be pushy and aggressive with someone you care about.

Instead, stay positive and support the advisor as they explain the process. Quill any uptight moments, providing moral support to the potential customer. Our job at that time is to reassure our friends and family members that this is the right choice for them, and can help them improve areas of their life.

2. Lead generation.

How does a successful multi level marketing company develop customers? There are several different ways to start building a customer base, and they all require lead generation. The customer in any sales industry starts out as a lead, or a person or business potentially interested in the product or service being sold. Without leads, success is likely not going to occur.

How do you find leads? There are several different ways to go about locating potential leads. The traditional way was door to door by foot, but thanks to telephones and digital marketing (which we will touch on in the next chapter), that is not the only way to achieve success. The next oldest way to acquire successful leads is to contact future clients via telephone, or telemarketing.

This is done by calling the clients and pitching the product or service while staying just vague enough to open the door for the actual sales appointment, unless you can close the deal via phone, which takes great skill and practice. These are the traditional ways to contact a lead, a phone call followed up by a personal visit.

One can make cold calls or get a list from a marketing provider of a specific area, age group, etc. The information is available is we look for it. Another great traditional method is the use of brochures, flyers and other forms of mail in offers. Traditional MLMs would provide the potential customer with information they just didn't think they could live without. The customer might fill out the form and send it back in, or call the number readily available on the printed material. Printed material is a great way to insure that the perspective customer has an interest in the product or service, because they filled out the form or made the initial call. We have to keep that interest going and increase it to be successful in the traditional ways.

Lead generation is the breath of life in an MLM. The more leads generated, the greater the potential number of sales. It is common knowledge that the more sales, the more success for the company. Realistically, it is a numbers game, so the more leads one has, the greater the chance of success.

3. Opportunity sharing and Products presentation.

This will be mostly the advisor's job. Opportunity sharing is a big part of sales. Perhaps one of the team is having a rough go of it. Sometimes simply providing them with a quality lead can be just the boost that a person needs to get back on top again. Being a team player can really benefit the team in general, and everyone needs a little help once and again. That is part of being an advisor too, sharing and preparing the team for the multi level marketing industry. We cannot always be the top sale person every month… or can we?

You have to vision yourself to become an advisor should you want to go full force. Learn everything about what you are selling, from the product specifications, multiple uses, warranty, and any potential problems. Once you know everything, you will be capable of answering any questions the potential client may have about it. A good MLM person will know everything there is to know about the products, services and compensation plans. If you stutter, or stammer, or do not show complete competence it can eliminate the sale before you get halfway through a presentation. Potential customers won't make a purchase unless the person presenting the product has confidence in it.

Presentation is not everything, but it is a big part of the package. When you are looking to purchase a new car, think about it like going to 2 different dealerships. The first dealership points to the car on the lot and tells you to go take a look. They don't hand you the keys, or walk out with you. They sit, with their feet propped on the desk sipping a Big Gulp. The second lot you visit, you find yourself greeted with a smile. The sales person meets you, asks what you are interested in, and picks up several sets of keys. They then escort you to the lot, telling you all aspects of the vehicle, offering a test drive. Same price, and the same car. Which one are you going to choose, the one who presented the car, or the one that just pointed you in the right direction? Most people would go with the friendlier of the two that took the time to show the vehicle. That is the type of sales person an MLM representative should be. That is what we are, and what a new successful multi level marketing representative must become.

4. Product of your product

We become a product of our product, whatever it may be. We live, breath and become a part of whatever it is we are promoting and selling. Why? Confidence in a product creates sales. That means we have to be so much a part of the product that no one questions our faith in its functionality. Of course, this can only be a reality if our product deserves our embellished attentions.

This is why multi level marketing companies that are successful only promote quality products that deserve such praise and loyalty. This doesn't mean you ignore all other aspects of life, as that can suck the joy right out of waking up each day. So, no, we become a part of our products, and they become a part of us while we continue living life. The joy of an MLM is the freedom to enjoy life without all the hustle and bustle of a nine to five grind.

Being a product of one's product is a good thing. It is what provides us with a paycheck. It is what causes our face to shine with health and beauty. Our confidence allows our team to be confident. One cannot be involved in sales and be successful without being competent and confident, aka a product of your product.

5. Follow up and follow through.

One of the biggest mistakes an MLM sales person can make is to not follow up on a lead. Any lead has potential, and to ignore that potential is a fatal sales error. One thing you learn after years of working in the multi level marketing industry is that there are no definite fails or definite sales. The least likely client can actually be the biggest sale. On the same note, the most highly anticipated sale can occasionally fall through. The old saying never put all your eggs in one basket will most certainly apply in the world of sales.

It is also of the utmost importance that the sales persons always follow through with any appointments, obligations or promises to any potential clients… and the team. One of the quickest ways to lose future sales is by telling a perspective client you will do something, and then not following through. It is amazing how quickly word can spread in the industry that a sales person not reliable, or doesn't keep his word. Not only will an individual like that not make a lot of sales, they will also not be a very sought after team member in the multi level media community.

The two top rules for any sales person, after being confident and knowing about the product that makes your paycheck, is to follow up and follow through. That applies in any sales industry from MLMs to car sales, but don't be pushy. There is an etiquette to following up with your perspective clients that one most adhere too. Being a pushy salesman is a quick way to get an interested client to clam up and feel pressured. Pressure will sometimes make those clients say no, even if they really want to say yes. The right follow up can be the difference in a sale and a fail, so if you remember nothing else, remember that.

It may seem that all multi level marketing companies are just cookie cutter copies of one another, but that isn't the case. Just because an MLM has a traditional structure doesn't mean it is exactly like all the others. Lots of companies have the same structure but are very different. The motivation of the individuals involved can be a real dynamic within the organization. The product is also very important, along with the team's faith in the items involved.

You cannot judge a book by its cover, nor can you judge a multi level marketing company by its structure. The traditional methods of running an MLM have been proven tried and true over the decades. The difference in a successful and an unsuccessful company can sometimes be the steps involved in making it great. There is no shame in utilizing a structure that is proven as reliable, such as the system listed in this chapter.

The steps are simple and proven. They have worked for multi level marketing companies year after year. The products and teams eventually change, but the system stays true. Successful MLMs will follow the ABC's, become an advisor, build a bridge and start drawing in customers. The successful sales persons will then generate leads, follow up on those leads and follow through with any obligations made. The team will know the product, inside and out. There will be no question they cannot answer, and no rebuttal one cannot rebuke. The sales will start to stack up and money will roll IF you follow these simple steps.

It isn't difficult to get an MLM on top if you really put effort into it. Don't be one of those sales persons that expect the sales to just flock your way. Instead, go out and look, participate in events, and start walking on the road to success. There is nothing quite like the success that comes with a traditional MLM network marketing business opportunity.

New Age Marketing Workshop

Notes

4. MLM THE NEW AGE WAY

There are traditional ways to handle multi level marketing as we discussed in chapter 3, but the digital age has really opened a lot of opportunities for sales people with quality products. There are so many new outlets that allow us to jump into the future with our potential clients.

Sometimes I feel sorry for the MLM teams before the digital era. Those guys had it pretty tough, and they had additional costs. Instead of email, they used snail mail, spending money on postage. Instead of speaking to the clients via social media, they had to travel out physically to present the products. It was like the Neanderthal age of sales, as far as marketing capability. Now, speaking to a client or promoting a product is as easy as 1, 2, 3.

1. Facebook.

Facebook is not just about chatting with friends anymore. It has became an additional face for businesses, sales persons and multi level marketing teams all across the world. Facebook is just one of many social media options that we can take advantage of. It is being utilized for so many reasons other than just friendships now.

There are an abundance of businesses that utilize Facebook to promote products, services and provide the company or sales representative with a pleasant social face. It can give a sales person a more human face, and a friendlier persona. This is a way to show perspective clients that we are just normal people, working to make a living and enjoy a life with our families. Some individuals will occasionally put something personal, like the birth of a child, or a graduation, just to allow clients to see them as more personable. It is an amazing opportunity to make friends, and clients.

As a promotional tool, Facebook can become an amazing asset. It is a good showplace for premiering products. You can post positive reviews from clients about your products and services. People love to know what other people think, and posting reviews is a wonderful outlet resource to utilize. People can post a review directly to the page itself. This allows anyone who visits your page to see what wonderful things people have to say about exactly what it is you represent. A Facebook page can start out slow and build over time. As the followers build, so does the audience that will be viewing the product. In the MLM industry, this can be the beginning of beautiful, professional relationships.

Hashtags can also be utilized on Facebook.

2. Social Media

Facebook is just one example of social media. The power of social networking is truly phenomenal. Social media is not something to be overlooked or underestimated in the multi level marketing industry. It is an amazing array of digital access and platforms that allow different types of representation from a full business profile to short clips and statements. Some of the best platforms to consider are:

LinkedIn. This is a fantastic place to put a professional profile and make professional and business connections. LinkedIn is the business man and women's social media site for networking and making connections all around the world.

Twitter. This site is great for a mini profile that can post a multitude of short statements regarding promotions, sales, new products, new team members, and links. Twitter is one of the most popular social platforms available and is widely used by celebrities, businesses, marketing professionals, and people in general. You can search for specific entities and hashtag out a Tweet that will pop directly on their page. It is a wonderful marketing tool.

Tumblr. This is a small profile social platform that allows the posting of videos, links, articles, images and other information. It is somewhat like Facebook, as far as what can be posted, though it is a pretty straight forward site. It does appear to have less bugs than Facebook, and seldom gets a lot of robotic ads posted. It allows for hashtags and can be easily posted to other social media sites.

Google Plus, aka G+. Google has made several attempts in the social media realm, but G+ is the most successful so far. Yes, it has glitches but they aren't too severe in most cases. The worst aspect of this platform is the jumbled way in which information is seen. Notifications are given, but instead of a scroll by date option, everything is scattered on a page of endless scrolls. It is a nice addition but shouldn't be used as a primary social media platform.

YouTube is another great platform to utilize. Making a "how to" video can be a wonderful way of gaining potential customers. It allows your audience to easily visualize the product. If we do it ourselves, it adds a human side to any sales pitch we might use. People like to see a product they are considering in use. A video makes the product a usable object instead of just an object. YouTube is compatible with each one of the other social networks if not by embed, then by link. It can be an amazing asset to utilize, and is a highly recommended tool for increasing sales in the network marketing industry.

Hadoop is a great platform to use for posting multi marketing posts directed to different social media networks. It can be utilized with Twitter, Facebook and other sites to post up pre scheduled data. This is a wonderful convenience for the busy MLM representative and allows diligent postings for up to several weeks in advance. It is a very convenient addition to the social media business world.

3. Email Marketing.

Social media also allows us to publically post our email for potential clients to see. This raises our potential to get interested clients to contact us. We should always, always, always cross post the same email address consistently. This just makes life less complicated.

Another way to utilize email is to have interested parties request information via the clicking or unclicking of an ad, or other method, including lead generated interest. We can then add them to an email list, and send out the information on a weekly or monthly basis. You don't want to blast emails daily, as often this leads to the spam folder.

Always have an unsubscribe button somewhere in your ad. It doesn't have to be bright and draw attention, it should just exist. This lets your perspective clients know that your confident enough in your products that they have the option of unsubscribing from the great deals your about to provide them with. It is a very passive aggressive marketing technique.

4. Lead Generation.

Something all multi level marketing or network marketing professionals need to remember is without leads, there is no sales funnel. Lead generation is extremely important and we have to utilize every available option in today's digital world. We can contact anyone, anywhere via the internet.

In the MLM industry, we live on leads. A lead is the direct path to our clients, which lead to our financial security, and social media offers us a God like advantage over the sales days of old. Each form of social media listed from Facebook to Twitter is like opening a gate straight to a customer's door. Social media allows us to send video, images, links, marketing options, specials, and all varieties of information in order to draw in a larger cliental. The more channels we use, the more opportunities that can arise.

Social media is the way to get to a larger client base in a much shorter amount of time, especially if you are using a platform like Hadoop. The more information you get out about the products and services available, the more leads you will generate. You can do online chats with customers, throw surveys out, post ads and promotions.

To generate leads we have to make ourselves accessible and contact potential customers back when they email or instant message us. We don't just get leads, we have to follow up on leads. When we take the time to talk to people online, they will be more likely to consider the MLM for a business opportunity. Good communication makes a good lead. Good leads will lead us to an eventual sale. Multi level marketing companies are all about sales and return business relationships.

Leads can also be generated from previous customers. We have to maintain a level of trust with our clients. When it comes to sales, you don't want to break the trust or product quality, else future sales could falter. Many a fabulous sales person has gotten greedy and let quality slide, only to be seen working in a car lot later in the future. That will never happen if you adhere to the guidelines that I used to become successful in the multi level marketing industry.

5. Attraction Marketing.

The term attraction marketing took a grand stand in the network marketing scene a few years back and mesmerized an entirely new generation of multi level marketing professionals. The new terminology took the focus off the product and put it on the team member, and the company they happen to be representing in the industry. No longer must we attempt to manipulate people into trusting new products, or even to garner faith in a new company that no one has ever heard anything about.

Instead, we want them to focus on us. We are the star that is shining brightly and keeping their attention. We are here to guide them, and help them find qualified results and lucrative business ventures for today and in the future. A skilled attraction marketer in today's industry does several different things to seal the deal and keep customers interested and happy.

What is attraction marketing? The person as the attraction point in the marketing. The success of attraction marketing lies solely on that person's ability to attract, and maintain that attraction.

The first thing an attraction marketer should do is generate a continuous supply of high quality, responsive leads. After lead generation, the next step is to create a beneficial relationship with the leads. Be friendly, be receptive, be personable, and be honest. Always keep appointments and obligations that have been agreed upon. The next step is to embrace the system and generate income from leads that have been garnered, and keep it going in a residual fashion. A lead doesn't have to end with just one stop… This is not the quickie mart. The key step is to benefit others who embrace the system and all the opportunities involved.

We have to utilize internet marketing to offer the right information and catch the attention of all those potential customers, just waiting to hear about us. The online data is our way to reach out and establish our ability to shine in our current niche. Customers will read that information and react either by clicking on a different page, or, if you have created a skilled attraction marketing platform, they will show interest.

We want to provide them with a beautiful bounty of free information and high quality content. The purpose is to garner the trust of our clients, and to build our reputation in marketing based on that trust. If we maintain a factually secure presence, along with some charisma, we can truly be successful in the attraction marketing scene that is continuing to grow and evolve.

Traditional multi level marketing campaigns can be very beneficial, however, in my opinion, multi level marketing has more vantage points and opportunities with the new age way.

Digital technology has taken network marketing ahead for decades. The potential marketing and sales opportunities, the outreach, the ease of digital communication and even eCommerce has made the MLM industry run like a very smooth, efficient, well oiled machine.

From the perspective of someone who started at the bottom and soared to the top, I can say that the new age mulit level marketing capabilities have really improved over the years.

When looking back on the technology available a few decades ago, it is somewhat amusing to realize how easily we can now overcome obstacles like distance, and travelling short distances with no complications. Even ordering is done with ease thanks to the digital era, and social media can be a professional MLM team member's best friend if utilized correctly. Personally, I am grateful for the wonders of modern technology and the ease of digital marketing and sales. The online tools are limitless.

Trump Tower In New York

Notes

5. HOW TO CHOOSE A MLM

In the earlier days, when I first became interested in getting in to network marketing, the industry was quite different. The number of companies that were doing real multi level marketing were sparse, so people didn't have a lot to choose from. Even for those legitimate ones, the timing was not really right. No one really had to go on a big quest to find the right company, because the options were fairly limited in most areas, including my own. Today, things are a lot different, and in order to succeed in this market one has to really immerse themselves into discovering the roots of the network marketing professionals that they are considering.

Years ago, friends and family members who were involved in the MLM industry would provide a referral, reassuring us that we'd be in good hands with the company they were involved in. Due to the amount of tricky pyramid schemes that use to exist, many people fell prey to scams and found themselves seeking something better.

There are well over 3,000 network marketing companies, with more joining the ranks almost weekly. This doesn't mean that all those in business are professional MLMs. That makes it almost mandatory to delve into the history and business practices of the company being considered before making a commitment. You don't want to embrace a multi level marketing company that doesn't have an outstanding reputation. Working for the wrong company can make it more difficult to get a job with the right one. It is important to keep business dealings legitimate.

The history of a company is very important and should be an important part of the decision making process. How long have they been in business? Have there been complaints filed against the company with the Better Business Bureau or CASE? Have they been reviewed online via any of the sites, like Yelp? Check out websites, social media, reviews about the company and the products they sell… then look at how your life could be if you chose to become a part of the company. You decision can either help make your dreams come true, or cause you to revert back to a previous lifestyle. Think clearly, ponder everything and evaluate every angle.

Here are 5 aspects of an MLM to evaluate before joining the company:

1. Training.

What type of training is available for new team members? Some companies provide DVDs or pre-recorded material. Some direct you to a website where you will read information and watch a video. Others have you come into an office to once again, watch a DVD.

There are MLM conventions that we can attend to learn more. Will the company pay for part of the cost, or are we responsible for it all. Is the price reasonable, like $50 or so? Do they include a new employee kit of some type and how much does it cost. The options for training are unlimited when you consider digitally accessible options.

Training and understanding is important in the industry. Knowledge of the product is a much in order to be successful in sales. What type of enlightenment and product information is included? Listen to all the information involved, and check out the product completely to make sure it is something you are comfortable selling and promoting.

2. Coaching and Mentoring.

The coach and mentor is an important part of choosing the right multi level marketing firm. A good coach and mentor can take even the weakest link in the marketing chain and make them a top seller in a limited amount of time, as long as the individual has the drive and desire to succeed.

A coach and mentor is a supportive, enlightening individual with epic skills who once stood in your shoes as a new team member. They worked hard to succeed, grow, and rise up in the ranks to become who they are today. Now, they take new MLM representatives and share all the knowledge gained over years in the industry. They answer questions, provide support, and help to home in on the skills, strengths, and weaknesses of members, helping them to improve in all areas.

Just like in our youth, the good coach and mentor can become an important part of our lives and the journey. This time, they will be helping to make our dreams come true. However, it is up to us to be motivated, follow those instructions, take in the knowledge, and move forward with it. The coach and mentor is here to help, but new team members have to be receptive and coachable.

Mentoring is just as important as coaching. Both are important aspects of early development, and our skills later in life. Even Forbes has posted information in regards to the importance of mentors in the business. My own mentor was a life saver, helping me start taking initiative to evolve into the mentor I am today.

Network marketing has worked mentoring and coaching right into the very foundation of the business. Everything begins with our products, or services in some cases. Sales start the wheel turning, and the team members are the spokes of that wheel. The one person recruits a team, coaches and mentors that team. The team is then encouraged to become coaches or mentors themselves. More new team members are hired in under the new coaches and team members, and the wheel continues to turn. The top tier mentors get overriding off all the tiers below them, but everyone on the team benefits from sales in some way. A mentor earns excellent commissions, especially with a happy, motivated team.

3. Company Background.

The company background is a very important aspect when looking at an MLM. There are a multitude of ways to check out a new business before diving in and signing a contract. There are good and bad network marketing businesses in the industry today. Some have been around a while, but multiple new businesses are joining the market monthly. These are some of the best ways to really investigate a multi level marketing company.

Contact the Better Business Bureau if you are in USA or the CASE if you are in Singapore. See if the company has had any reports filed against them. Get information on the actual complaint to ensure its legitimacy and evaluate the seriousness of the issues. If there are multiple complaints filed against the MLM being considered… it is likely not a company you want to join the ranks of.

Facebook. This social media network allows businesses to get comments and reviews. Taking the time to read over this section of a potential MLMs page can be extremely enlightening. You can get a view of the business via the customer's perspective. You can also see how they evaluate the products being sold, and how social media is utilized for sales.

LinkedIn. This professional website can give you an idea of the company you are considering also. It is easy to observe how often the profile is updated and the type of information published. Check out some of the connections, as we learn early on one can be judged by the company kept.

Website. Check out the company website. Do they have a customer comment section? What about company policies on returns and dissatisfaction? How do they treat unhappy clients. A website should be an excellent representation of a business's public face. It should never be the only option utilized, but it is a good resource to balance out with social media and the Better Business Bureau.

4. Compensation Plan, Reward System and Bonuses.

There are a variety of different compensation plans available for multi level marketing companies, which we will further describe in Chapter 6. The primary types of payment plans are Powerline, Uniline, Binary, and the Matrix. Each of these plans has strengths and weaknesses, but they all offer fair, compatible payment plans. Payments can be based on commission, or a set fee per sale, or fee per amount. In most cases, whatever the compensation plan is, it will by far exceed any standard 9 to 5 job in the industry. Hard work gets high rewards when it comes to network marketing. Reward systems and bonuses are another useful way the networking marketing companies help to compensate the team members. The reward systems vary according to company. Some MLMs will give a financial bonus in the form of an additional percentage for outstanding sales, or just a specific figure based on the amount of the sale. Still other multi level marketing companies will provide rewards in the form of a paid vacation, weekend trip, or even a car. Reward and bonus systems may vary, but rest assured, they are impressive addition to the compensation packages in most cases.

5. Leadership.

Leadership material in the industry is someone who comes in and is so motivated, they motivate others. This type of individual will encourage the team to do better as a whole. A leader will sometimes sacrifice credit for someone else in order to inspire more from that individual.

A leader embraces a performance review based on the entire team, not their actions alone. A real leader in the network marketing industry has the capability to create an excellent residual income within around 18 months due to the sheer focus and efforts that they put into the sales, AND creating and building additional teams. A leader is an inspiring teacher, trainer and coach.

An MLM leader should have a massive vision of what they want the future to hold. It should be decided during the first week. They should understand the product knowledge is not performance, but is only an enhancement, and share this with team members. Understand and share that compensation plan information is irrelevant when it comes to performance. A leader should have a daily routine with social media and sales and stick to it.

A good leader might make a training list for new team members to aid in training. One doesn't get to stressed when someone doesn't perform as expected. The team has to be inspired, not worried about a stressed out team mate.

A leader will set goals and hit those goals, and lead by example. One cannot expect a team to be loyal and stick to hitting the numbers if one doesn't do it also. Goals are very important to the success of the team, uplines and downlines. A good leader doesn't forget to ask questions also. Be respectful and take an interest in the team so you can better inspire them. Inspiration is another tool for success, both with the team and with perspective customers.

Everyone has a slump, but leaders maintain motivation. A good leader will further their own training to improve in any areas where they could be lacking. Sometimes one has to just roll up those sleeves and focus on the business to improve. We also never want to do or say anything we wouldn't want our team to repeat. That may sound a bit like parenting, but it is just MLM leadership.

A good leader keeps living the leadership lifestyle and setting an example for the network marketing team. We will optimize every advantage available from traditional marketing means to the wondrous access of social media, digital and mobile technology. I decided to be a leader that led by example, and it is a code I've continued throughout my career.

Joining a multi level marketing group is a commitment to work hard and move forward in the fast lane. There is no slow lane in the industry. In the words of the renowned Hunter Thompson, "buy the ticket, take the ride," aka go for the gusto and be all you can be in the industry. We are only limited by our own decisions, and the network marketing industry gives us full access to be whatever we choose. We can make as much or as little as we wish, but no salesman ever said, I want a small paycheck.

The MLM industry is a fascinating business to be in, especially in today's day and age. Things have improved so much over the decades a professional sales person has to put more effort into failing than success. If you have been considering getting involved in the multi level marketing business, follow these simple steps, work hard, and you will find yourself living the dream… just like I did.

What industry leader Ben Low says...

The truth is not everyone will succeed.

MLM is a great system, but you got to know how to use it to help yourself and the people around you.

Lets take a double-edged sword, whether it will benefit or harm you, it depends on how you utilise it.

If you are just a Salesman, MLM just mean Multi-Level Marketing to you. To me, I take on the role of a mentor, so MLM means Multi-Level Management or Multi-Level Mentorship because I am responsible for their success as long as you have the hunger to succeed.

We equip everyone with the necessary skills and knowledge to succeed and want to dispel the myth that you will earn once you join us.

To be an effective leader, you got to be a great manager or mentor and Make Life Meaningful. If not, it will be Make Life Miserable.

2 person in the same team can have differing results, so the issue lies with the person and not with the system.

We as leaders and mentors create conducive environment to help people succeed, but people got to help themselves succeed too.

People question why do I need to move into an office, any room with tables and chairs will be enough to do training. I want to invest in my team to repay their belief in me and this is what makes us different.

I earn around 120 thousands in 6 months, and I am concerned about how they can earn the same amount as me. I am not interested about how much commission I can squeeze from them but I will ask them how much do they want to make in 6 months and work towards the goal together.

As a tip to anyone looking to join a Network Marketing team, you have got to find out and join one that provides training. You have to also look for mentors who are independent and not reliant on piggybacking.

You also have to understand if you are a risk taker. If you are, aim to be the first person or '001'. It is a very tough position because you have to start everything from scratch but the rewards are very lucrative.

Even if your income is the same as when you are employed, your lifestyle here is much more relaxing. If you choose not to work today, you will still earn an income.

Ben Low

Email : blbsmlm@gmail.com
Mobile : 65 97986655

6. COMPENSATION PLAN

We all have to make a living in some way and multi level marketing companies are the same. What makes the compensation for network marketing stand out is the structure varieties that sales persons in the industry can receive.

Different MLMs pay in different ways, and some of them are really unique. In order to run a successful MLM, we have to determine the best complete compensation package to offer. There are plenty of "how to" guides on line, but in most cases, they are incomplete, or lack all the relevant information necessary to succeed in such a competitive industry. In most cases people do not want to tell you the whole story on how to recreate the success they themselves have. Why? Usually, they do not want to share the stage, even if the products are different. They might tell you 8 out of 10 steps to make an outstanding company. Rest assured, they will leave out a few of the most important bits of information.

In this book, I am giving you the best of the best information available, especially in regards to compensation plans.

Payment plans will either be the nail in the coffin for a business, or it can be the star that shines above all other MLMs. It completely depends on the business structure and financial plan that you have envisioned to achieve the luxury lifestyle you want to enjoy. You never want to under compensate quality team members, but at the same time, overcompensating can quickly get you into a hole that won't be easy to crawl out of. There is no greater illusion than one of self, yet un-obtained grandeur. We should never extend ourselves beyond the means proven capable, and all goals should stay within the borders of reality. As an example, do not anticipate making a million dollars in sales your first week. It is good to set a higher than average goal, but never set a higher than able to achieve goal. Some owners get stars in their eyes, get lost in the moment, and don't look at substantiated capabilities.

They push too hard, and can drive team members away by expecting too much and paying too little. Having confidence in one's capabilities is a must, but don't allow that confidence to exceed realistic expectations. We want to motivate, inspire, and give financial compensations that will give team members the inspiration necessary to succeed in the multi level marketing industry. The first step to creating a viable compensation plan is to understand exactly how compensation works in the network marketing world. Study each type thoroughly and make sure you have complete knowledge of the individual structures and exactly what they could mean for your MLM.

Look at other successful businesses in the same field and the type of payments they offer their team, but make sure and examine the trust levels as well. The compensation may look good but the company's reliability may not. After all that, you need to make sure the compensation plan you are offering falls under all the legal guidelines that are currently being enforced. The laws can change overnight in some cases, and a new network marketing company never wants to get caught in that kind of crossfire. Without proper research, you might find yourself being labeled as a pyramid scheme, so take the time to find out accurate information, and all the legalities of the day. The purpose in chapter 6 is to take a look at each individual pay structure, including the positive and negative aspects.

There are many different types of compensation plans widely used by MLMs. The ones that I am going to touch on include Binary, Unilevel, Matrix, Powerline. They each have unique aspects that encourage us to consider the possibilities and the potential within each system.

1. Binary

Binary compensation is one of the most popular forms of payment in the multi level marketing industry. Distributors absolutely love the Binary structure, and give is buzz word references, like the payment plan that sizzles. The set up is that each distributor can only have 2 first level team members at any given time, but there is no limit in how many levels there can actually be, only on the number of persons per level.

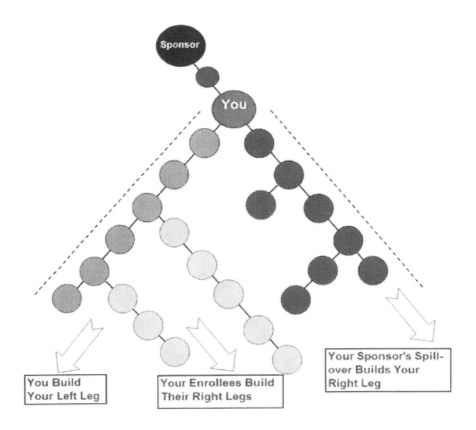

It has been confused with a "2 times infinity" matrix plan, but it is not really that familiar. It simply gets mislabeled because of the 2 limit on the first level. There are basically 2 parts to the binary plan. The left and right parts of the compensations, but the parts can grow and evolve on both the inner and the outside. The outside is often referred to as the "power leg" as it automatically benefits from new distributor placement from all upline levels of the MLM. The inner is sometimes called the inside leg, aka profit area. It is the distributors we pick, and there are limitations. The binary commission is normally based on total business volume points, not the actual levels.

Commissions are formula dependent on both inside and outside areas. MLMs use to insist the two levels matched, but that can be very tedious. In modern times they will balance it out if one side makes ¼ and the other makes ¾ in sales, the sales staff makes a commission equal to the percentage of the lesser volume.

Thus, it is important to balance the binary plan on both sides. Sales always get the percentage lesser than, so making the 2 areas balance equals better pay.

The advantages of the binary plan are the spillover, from the upline, as it can be profitable. The disadvantages are also the spillover, as one starts to count on that. It makes it hard to recruit and keep first lines happy.

You don't want to be on the inside. The binary plan makes each sales team member responsible for their own actions and finances. They do so by recruiting and sponsoring others. The sponsored members will help lead one another and the recruiting team member to new financial heights, if everyone works hard to meet and succeed in reaching goals. Additional team members fall onto the power side, and become part of the spillover, which can be beneficial. This happens regardless of which team member did the recruiting. There can be only two…

2. Unilevel.

Some people see the Unilevel compensation plan as the best option when it comes to network marketing. Why? For the most part, it allows us to control our income based primarily on our own efforts. One example of this would be as follows: I collect 12 new customers and get paid $100 each, totaling $1200. If I can get these same customers to sign up for monthly orders, it will create a residual income. It would only be a fraction of the initial payment, probably around 5% to a high of 30%, dependant on the structure. I might make a reasonable income on that percentage, but I made more on the initial sale. This alone should motivate me to get out and keep adding customers to get the higher payment of $100.

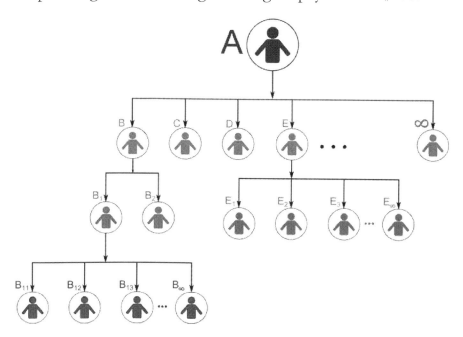

The unilevel compensation system is a simple plant that has a single line of sponsors; we build a strong network, and create a dedicated first level of distributors. Level ranks are almost irrelevant with this system, which make some network marketers very happy. One member can sponsor a single vendor to create a team that all receive the same level of compensation. This maintains a balance and all the first levels get paid the same. It is simplified. The problem can be in the recruiting, as this system keeps things balanced, and many network marketers prefer to have a limitless cap on payment opportunities. The cap involved in this system makes bringing in more motivated sales persons a bit difficult. Another downside is that this compensation plan puts the lines against the distributors in competition, which can prove to cause some tensions. On a positive note, this is a straightforward compensation option where pay is somewhat fair across the board. The distributors that make more sales and receive the same compensation may not agree, but those who try, but don't quite reach targets will be thrilled.

3. Matrix.

The forced matrix structure sets boundaries from the beginning with width and depth matrix. An example would be a 5 by 3 structure would have the distributors sponsoring 5 additional individuals, and profits would be gained from 3 levels deep for those recruited. This plan allows MLMs to benefit from spillover by consistently adding new recruits under the primary distributors within those 3 levels.

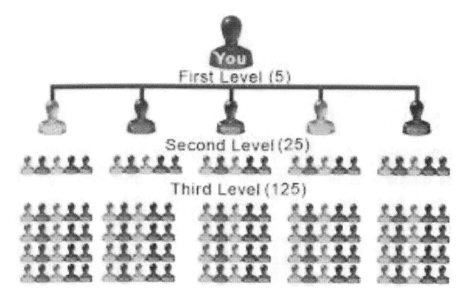

This structure does give the distributors a lot of control, but it also promotes team work and everyone getting a fair share. It is basically similar to a unilevel plan but the primary focus is on limiting width and limited depth. The first number refers to the width of the plan with the second referring to the depth. If you think you might enjoy working a matrix, just take the number of distributors and multiply them by the number on the previous depth.

The potential size of the matrix doesn't mean a lot to a distributor. What does mean a lot is having an understanding as to how this type of pay plan works. You have to be able to understand the operation in order to run a sustainable marketing business. The overall success of any marketing plan depends on one's own character and the nature of the products being sold. That means you need to determine what type of distributor you are going to be, and will you use the product as well? Are you a recruiter, sales leader, or just a sales team member?

You need to be motivated to succeed in this type of pay plan structure. This structure is best suited for companies with sales staff that wants to switch up to coaching relatively quickly. The pros of the matrix system are mostly in the teamwork it inspires. This allows distributors and the team in general, to remain a part of the company for many years. After a first line is filled, the distributor can more easily focus on motivation and training tools to keep the team inspired.

The training and motivational ability with this system is top notch. The downside of the matrix system is the stagnantation that can come from limited growth and earning cap. You can only make so much with this type of structure. There can be other programs implemented to compensate for the cap. Some companies create bonus programs and other motivational payment options and awards to encourage veteran team members to keep on, keeping on. It allows these hard earners to gain extra income beyond the matrix plan

4. Powerline

The powerline compensation plan is another simple plan related to MLMs. It is based on giving and getting returns. For instance, in previous years, I could pass up a sale or 3 to one of my sponsors. I give away a few sales. However, after doing so, every member of my referred team does the same for me. I could end up with 12 or more sales just for giving up 3. We have all heard the expression, "you get what you give." With the powerline compensation plan you get more than you give, because you get it from every member of the team. The downline team members that pass up to you through the powerlines fall under tier 1 sales. This will not appear unless you have also accrued powerline sales.

As the powerlines or legs sides grow, level 2 grows, followed by level 3, than level 4, and so on. Another example would be the 2 up program, which is common. Each member will have 2 sales passed up by the script toward the sponsors above them. From that point forward, all sales come back to them, along with referrals, and the referrals of referrals. It is an amazing turnaround opportunity and a very positive pay plan.

Autoship and **DSA** are also terms where you need to understand when delving into the world of multi level marketing. Let's discuss below.

1. Autoship

The Autoship structure is still utilized and is an important part of a successful network marketing plan. It has been the gold star standard and a very relevant process in the multi level marketing industry for a very long time. An autoship is the act of automatic purchase every month. For instance, your customer activate autoship and purchase $300 worth of products for consumption on a monthly basis, you will have $300 sales recurring every month !

This can be great if you are capable of selling that package for the prices estimated. You can then make your money back tenfold with the right attitude and attraction marketing.

Initially, the entire concept of autoship can seem a little troubling. After all, you are committing to a monthly bill in order to generate income. However, after becoming more familiar with the way multi level marketing companies work, the entire autoship process became a lot more understandable.

When using autoship, the team members get the convenience of receiving the packages in a timely manner, and not having to wait on products can be a life saver. If you like your product and actively use it, the autoship can be a real lifesaver. The product will be there on time, every month and you, nor will your clients ever have to wait on things like that. The autoship will keep you actively maintaining a quality supply of the product. Using the product also gives an advantage, as customers can often tell a real testimonial from a faux review. It helps us familiarize ourselves with the products, and have them as a part of our lives.

However, if the customer cancels an order, or decreases the volume, the responsibility of payment falls on the sales team member. We do not get to alter any numbers involved with the autoship contract. What happens if you don't make your sales back? Are you compensated, or expected to purchase a package the following month?

This can go both ways, and the drawbacks of an autoship plan can be far worse than the benefits are great. If a sales person is in a slump, and doesn't make any sales for a period of several months, they can end up deeper in debt than when they started network marketing. The definition of autoship is getting products shipped at specific times to a specific location.

This is what we love getting our clients to do, sign up for repeat business. It is great when they do so, but for us it can really cause some challenging sales, especially around the holidays and specific times of year. Those that fall behind have to keep paying will find their financial situation plummeting into a realm they'd prefer to avoid.

The prepaid structure usually is rigid, lacking any room for error. Once agreed upon, the shipping will continue until the contract is terminated completely.

2. DSA.

The Direct Selling Association (DSA) is the national trade association for companies that offer entrepreneurial opportunities to independent sellers to market and sell products and services, typically outside of a fixed retail establishment. More than 20 million Americans are involved in direct selling in every state, congressional district and community in the United States. In 2015, direct selling generated more than $36 billion in retail sales.

What is direct selling? It is exactly what a network marketing or multi level marketing company is set up to do. We market and sell products from a specific location, be it a website online in this wondrous, digital age, or from a specific location. The oldest known example of direct sales was called peddling, like street peddlers, and peddlers at a bazaar or market back in the ancient times. It might have been homemade breads or simply potatoes. Today's DSA comes in several different structures, the one on one demonstration, a part plan, and personal contact via other means, such as internet marketing and eCommerce.

The direct sales structure is the favored industry for

independent sales persons. Over 77% of DSA members are labeled as MLM companies. After decades of obscurity, in the world of Multi level marketing, it seems what was once part time sales have rapidly became a full time position. Direct sales in today's world are far easier than those who have peddled in the past. Not only do we have traditional means of marketing, but direct sales on the internet and mobile devices allows us to get out products out and available with a lot less efforts than a backpack, or mule pulling a wagon.

We can utilize a website, or one of the selling sites like Amazon or Ebay now, creating pages of product on official eCommerce sites is a real game changer for the direct sales market. There are some famed direct sales companies out there that have been around for years. Some of the more renowned are Avon and Mary Kay, but even professional sales representatives for places like John Deere might have a product page available on one of the larger eCommerce sites like Amazon and eBay. There are so many options for direct sales associates to consider and utilize, one really has to put effort into failing. The art of direct sales has grown in leaps and bounds over the centuries, and this century is a beautiful time to take up the challenge of making your dreams come true. When it comes to network marketing compensation, there are a few things that need to be taken into consideration when creating a plan.

Pay in an MLM needs to be about more than just the sell, because most multi level marketing companies encourage team players. It is a good idea to award things like additional product purchases, selling outside the sales circle, inviting in new recruits, team building, training and supporting new recruits, evolving into a leader, and helping others to aspire to be leaders too.

Compensation should encourage all levels to meet and exceed sales goals, aspire to reach the top, stay active even during a great week, and not give up on a bad week. These are just a few considerations to ponder before making an official payment plan. The rewards should only be given to those who have gained recognition and influence, been promoted and continued to reach for the stars, has a noticeable hike in sales volume, encourages team motivation and increased sales, helps to increase the downline, and improve upon the multi level marketing company as a whole.

There are some things that all MLM beginners need to avoid when setting up a compensation plan. Do not make the qualifications to be awarded compensation too high, nor should you make them too low. They have to be enticing without seeming to good to be true, or inaccessible without overzealous goals. When someone does something phenomenal, make sure there is a valid amount of recognition for an outstanding job. Everyone gets optimistic, but do not become the Sham WOW guy from the infomercials… we all know what happened to him.

Above all, when thinking of bonus, truly evaluate the depth of the task performed and reward it accordingly. A multi level marketing business really needs to offer a compensation plan that makes it stand out among its peers. It is a very competitive industry and other than reputation, commissions are usually the next thing that draws the attention of the perspective representative. If you want to create a sturdy foundation that will draw new team members, encourage team building and ranking, while benefitting all involved, review these options carefully and determine what will work best for the company you see in those dreams.

To recap this chapter, we reviewed the different types of compensation plans that are available to multi level marketing companies. Each one has a strong point and a weak point. Some of these variations in pay techniques have been around for decades, others are new versions of old ways, but they are all still utilized in one organization or another. Most of the compensation plans allow team members to increase the incomes via work ethic and personal effort.

When we work for/with or start a multi level marketing company, we are compensated for our product sales and that of our recruits. In some of the above structures, we also benefit from our recruit's recruits, and so on down the line. A few examples of that type of structure can be found in companies like Pampered Chef, Amway and Avon. Some companies offer bonuses like cars, or packages or even expense paid trips to those that excel in the industry. These trips and unique awards can sometimes be more popular than an actual money bonus.

Different companies offer these incentives to increase sales, and the awards are only given to top tier sales team members that work hard and excel in the industry. Legitimate network marketing firms do charge a small fee for startup kits, but that balance out when you review the compensation in most cases. If you don't create a payment structure that balances out in comparison to the fees, you shouldn't expect to see a supportive team member. It is very important that multi level marketing firms offer a fair payment plan for team members.

To do otherwise can cause one to find that they are labeled as a pyramid scheme, and that is not a place you want to be. The compensation plan is an important part of the draw to a network marketing company. Those interested in an MLM are usually drawn for the lifestyle, the luxury and the lavish life experiences that seem to come with hard work at legitimate MLMs. When starting a new venture, you want to make sure that the company you stand in front of offers legitimacy, especially fair compensation.

The Binary system is relatively popular, as it is based on twos and keeps everyone on a limitless limit, so to speak. You can keep stacking those twos and increasing compensation. The Unilevel pay structure gives the team's individuals the freedom to choose their own income. The harder you work, the more you get paid. It is a popular method of payment in the industry.

The multi level marketing companies of the digital age have things that we didn't have years ago, the ability to take care of payments without reporting into the office. We can now easily work, order products and be compensated all from our homes. There are several ways to actually receive compensation, like PayPal, direct deposit, BitCoin, and paper checks. The paper checks can take the longest to receive if waiting on snail mail, meanwhile a direct deposit or PayPal set up can be seen in the bank account within a matter of days.

Digital payments can be the best route to go in an MLM for swift compensation opportunities with minimal fees and no inconveniences. An network marketing company gains favor due to the luxurious lifestyle and high end payments. The paid trips to glorious places as a legitimate bonus structures can often times be a motivation in itself to consider signing on with an MLM company.

When evaluating the best payment plan for the direct sales industry of your choice, ponder each option carefully. Weigh the pros and cons based on what type of company platform your goals require. Each option also has unique ways to alter the program with bonuses, prizes and trips. What motivates you to really put in effort and succeed? Think about that while considering the compensation choices, and do what you must to see the company and yourself succeed.

Paid for incentive trip to Bahamas Atlantis Paradise Island

Notes

7. VISION FOR LIFESTYLE AND LEADERSHIP

Over the years, Multi-level Marketing (MLM) has been involved a lot of word of mouth. This strategy has been the weapon of success by a lot of entrepreneurs, businessmen and marketers. A lot of people have been spreading different information about MLM. But do all of the information being disseminated are true? Does this controversial approach really does scam people? Or is it just that other entrepreneurs or businesspeople take advantage of this technique to scam people?

Unfortunately, that part was true, wherein those marketers or business owners are the ones taking advantage of the opportunity to produce huge amounts of wealth through MLM. But let us not delve into that because we are here to discuss and to expound on our knowledge about this topic. A lot of people who are striving to be successful in terms of their financial capabilities are vying for the benefits MLM has to offer. Being successful does not come in a day, or in a week, or in a month. Success arrives in perfect timing. So while waiting for it, have yourself be prepared with a strong vision on your lifestyle and your leadership skills. In this chapter, I will offer you the best possible characteristics you can be equipped with to successfully fulfil the vision you have for your MLM career.

1. **Dreams and Goals**

A successful MLM career should start with setting the best dreams and goals you want achieved. The best performing entrepreneur, a businessperson or a marketer allow themselves to practice and apply Peter Drucker's concept of SMART objectives. If you have no idea what this means then allow me to. SMART is a mnemonic that stands for:

S – pecific

· It is important to have the idea do you want to achieve in your established business and up to what degree are you willing to work for it. To help you out with what specific concepts or ideas we should keep in mind, take note of the question-starters: What, Where, When, Who, Which and Why' these will help you be guided through your start-up business.

M – easurable

· The best goals created can be tracked or be measured. A key to a successful business should always answer the question: "How Many" or "How Much"

A – ction Oriented

· Practice what you preach. If you say you are going to do something, make sure it is done. Being able to finish the task as you have declared should also be characterized by results.

R – ealistic and Relevant

· Some people might have the misconception that in setting goals we have to dream for impossible ones. It is just as important for any successful marketers to have the trait of being realistic. Businesses created are not meant to fulfill fantasies. These are real and relevant ways to be a successful individual. So in creating the best strategies, one must keep it real and relevant.

T – Time Based

· Discipline is one of the best benefits of setting goals that can be offered. Start on asking yourself "When are you going to be able to finish it". Being able to finish a certain task you have created for according to the deadline you have made will let you have that discipline that will produce more business opportunities.

Since the best way to construct your success has been laid out. It is time to administer these characteristics and try to create specific goals for your career. It is vital to have two different types of goals in mind. Short-term and Long-term, the world of marketing can be a very big playing field to start on. But why do we have to establish different marketing goals? In all aspects of life, setting goals can turn something that cannot be seen, be visible. That is an idea created by Tony Robbins. Basically, having these objectives that needs to be met places a future successful person into the proper mindset in accomplishing tasks. And these tasks seem to be of the highest quality that can be produced. Financial achievement can be attained by mastering the different marketing goals that you have set.

2. Bring-out the Leadership in you by sharing it to others

Network marketing has evolved all throughout the years. But in order for this marketing strategy to be successful, it needs to have leaders, leaders that will turn their down-line into leaders as well to create more leaders. Leaders that will only create followers will not be a successful network marketing strategy for the long term. That is why you have to be able to create self-sufficient network marketers to maintain the best possible quality that can be spread out through the market. How do we create more leaders? That is by having a set of principles and qualities that should be equipped and be known for the ones who you will train. Here are 7 characteristics you can consider for a better leadership quality.

Possess a Powerful Vision

Leaders that are already successful should make more leaders that are bound to be outstanding as well. They should be able to spread their own vision to them.

Prioritize knowledge on your product

In network marketing, you should be able to market different products at ease. In able to do that, those who will train you should be able to teach you what are the things that need to be considered to have a successful product pitch to customers?

Be dedicated on your craft

Dedication is one of the keys in successful network marketing. Discover the most efficient routine you can create and have that applied in some of your product pitches. Being a leader requires you to be hands-on in trying out new things that will make your product be known in the market. After seeing your newly created routine work perfectly, have them thought on your apprentices that are soon to be leaders too.

Part of being dedicated as a network marketing leader is by creating a published step-by-step manual for your colleagues. It ensures better quality of teaching if they have their own set of guidelines on their hands.

Motivation is Key

Leaders should possess the best quality of motivation. This will fuel you through your journey in network marketing. Remove less functioning colleagues and be the one that trains people that will contribute a large amount of success to your team.

Issues, problems and other failures will always be part of the job. But a leader should know how to convert it into motivation to have it dealt with and then turn it to solutions.

Keep your feet on the ground

Some of the leaders forget the meaning of being humble. A successful leader that should train other future leaders should know how to ask from other experts' different opinions or criticism to further improve their selves. Only boastful ones will never ask for more learning even if they are on the top of the food chain and that should not be the case.

Be the best speaker you can be

Walking the talk is one of the best weapons to be successful in training people. The ability to effectively speak and present to your customers will dictate who you are as a network marketer. For everyone especially leaders who are in the industry of network marketing, the best way to create leaders us by being the best speaker you can ever be. Having this fulfilled will definitely produce a positive result because of the effectiveness of the training you have provided them.

Set the highest standards for your team

Being successful in network marketing needs to be geared with the highest standards possible. A leader should never look soft or weak in the eyes of their colleagues as this will entail disbelief to his capabilities. It is wise to keep your head up high no matter what you experience. This ability requires a lot of effort to be maintained that is why it is best to share this 'how-to' to your colleagues.

Having these skills equipped does not mean you can instantly become successful. You have to remember that you should start by imposing these traits regularly, on a daily basis. Keep walking the talk, and keep practicing what you preach as they may say. The most important part of being an MLM leader is by bringing out the leader in them.

3. How to Produce a Huge Sum of Wealth?

Network marketing is not just and never was just for the sake of promoting a certain product or a business. It is created to produce the highest profit we can attain. Who would want to create an MLM business without receiving the benefit of high-profit? No one does. To prevent that from happening, look through these things so that you will be aware and that you will not fail hardly in establishing an MLM business.

Brand Yourself

Branding is one of the keys to high-profiting MLM business as this separates your unique qualities to help you pitch different products and services you offer to people. The more unique your brand will be, the easier for you to penetrate on different consumers' hearts as they always look for something new. Fulfilling this desire for new products that give better quality than usual ones will generate customers that are loyal to you.

Who are your Prospects?

Just like any other things. Target market is the one that also fuels motivation for a business. The ability to distinguish your target audience for your product will help you focus on the different strengths that will support your product and different weaknesses that will be worn as your armor.

Establish a wide network

For network marketing, you will never produce wealth so large by having a small network. Equip yourself with skills that make you a great influencer. Hangout with the right people. Recruit the smartest way possible.

These 3 points should always be practiced by heart to be able to produce the most possible wealth you can receive. Be specific and just be dedicated in your work. Be patient no matter what happens, the time will come you will find your financial capability expand in the widest possible.

4. The Life of a Luxury and Prestige

MLM has been resided with different people who were really financially challenged but later become one of the top-earning individuals. These people thought they have no hope for attaining that dream goal of being rich, of being able to spend money without being thrifty. This lifestyle is one of the dreams everyone must have in their minds.

As Confucius said, 'Choose a job you love, and you will never have to work a day in your life'. Multi-level Marketing suits this concept as this is a great job to be part of that will ensure us with work that we will love. It is great having to see other people fulfill their dreams. It is better to have your dreams materialize. But it is best to make your dreams come true with the team you are actually part of. That network marketing group that is finding its way to provide success not just for the business but also for their selves.

Prestige can be acquired with a great chance when you are working in an MLM business. But do not expect you will have that lifestyle as soon as you step into the industry. You have to make your way through it. Start off by establishing a small network. This network you create dictates the number of possibilities you can pitch your product. If you have the chance to meet different people, then what are the chances you will run into possible customers that are living a life of prestigiously and a luxuriously. One of the end-goals you should set is by being on top of the societal class. Using MLM strategy will definitely help you obtain that title.

You have to remember that you should never suck-up on these people, because sucking up and on them will only start the death of your career. Be honest on what product you sell, be dedicated about it. Practice what you have learned from your trainer and apply the leadership skills that were mentioned. The best way to apply leadership skills is by sharing them to your colleagues. Soon enough, practicing all of these in proper discipline, you will find yourself having that prestigious title you have been so eager to have.

5. Recognition

The idea of being recognized, being identified and being accepted as a trustworthy MLM business is one of the rewards you can receive. Since most of this type of business are commonly scammers or hustlers, a successful MLM business should still be up and running for the long term. The perfect network marketing business should be known for how good you are, how smart you are and how trustworthy you are in the eyes of many consumers.

Recognition is the best motivation for any network marketing businesses, an additional fuel to the best quality of work that can be provided. Convert that positive energy into better quality of pitching and presentations. Soon enough you will find yourself having more loyal customers than you have envisioned. More loyal customers ensure higher profit and longer business lifespan.

Notes

8. WHY PEOPLE FAIL?

It's no big secret that MLM is a very controversial methodology in the marketing industry. It's even less of a secret that people who get into MLM schemes tend to come out on the losing side of it. In fact, independent studies have shown that over 90% of MLM practitioners will fail. So why is it that this controversial corporate scheme is continuing to draw in a lot of people despite the high failure rates? It's difficult a prime answer to this question, but a lot of it has to do with people just really overestimating their capacities for achieving success despite lacking the know-how. While confidence and self-esteem are admirable traits, they need to be backed up by proper information, analyses, and methodologies in order for success to follow suit. What this chapter seeks to discuss is the significant personality traits that are commonly trending among those who fail at MLM.

1. Settling for the Wrong Side of the ESBI Quadrant (Robert Kiyosaki)

Robert Kiyosaki is a prominent public figure who rose to fame as the author of the Rich Dad, Poor Dad series of books. He is also the founder of the Rich Dad Company, a private financial literacy education firm that caters to entrepreneurs and corporate players. His financial advice and commentary is heeded and approved by various academic figures and accomplished entrepreneurs all over the world. One of his most notable contributions to the world of financial literacy is the ESBI Quadrant which he introduced in his book, Rich Dad's Cashflow Quadrant. We are going to borrow some principles that were introduced by Kiyosaki to highlight some common flaws in MLM practitioners that could spell potential doom in their financial performance.

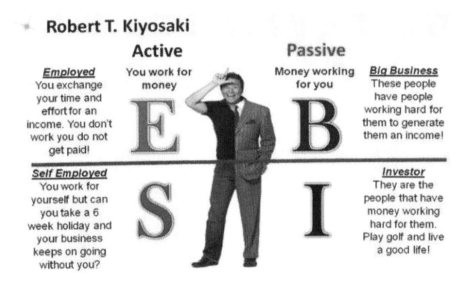

Understanding the Quadrants

Employee Quadrant (E)

The employee quadrant is where you will find a vast majority of corporate players. People who belong to this quadrant typically espouse the mindset of "I want a safe, secure, and comfortable job with great benefits." These are the people who will typically be working hard for a huge bulk of their days, and continue struggling to keep afloat in their lives of humble and "comfortable" means. Unfortunately for these people, their lack of drive and ambition to go beyond what is safe and comfortable entails that they are constantly having to rely on themselves alone to find success.

Self Employed Quadrant (S)

The members of the self-employed quadrant are people who are more ambitious and more daring in how they go about climbing the financial ladder. However, they are similar with those in the E Quadrant in the sense that they have high levels of self-dependence and self-reliance. The people you will find in the S Quadrant are typically those who have their own small businesses with less than 500 employees. They have the potential to be big, but their reluctance to delegate work and share responsibilities will ultimately leave them feeling burned out. More often than not, an S Quadrant member's business is likely to fall and crumble to ashes once the person on top chooses to take a short vacation or is forced to take a break.

Big Business Quadrant (B)

Similar to the inhabitants of the S Quadrant, people in the B Quadrant are also owners of their own businesses. However, they differ drastically in outlook and in methodology. Residents of the B Quadrant run businesses that employ more than 500 people. They are deeply committed to finding and gathering the right group of people to create an effective corporate machinery that does all the work on his behalf. The S Quadrant business owner is constantly stressed and busy working his days away overseeing the production of his business while the B Quadrant business owner is more engrossed with big picture analysis and doesn't have to slave over the nitty-gritties. The B Quadrant business owners run independent entities that can survive without him, but still work for his benefit.

Investor Quadrant (I)

The members of the investor quadrant take very cerebral approaches in their financial undertakings. In comparison with the others, the people in the I Quadrant are the ones offer the least amount of work, but in most cases, gain the most reward. People in the I Quadrant are financially literate and have a profound understanding of how money flows and how they can employ this knowledge in ways that benefit them.

So while E Quadrant member is slaving away at his cubicle, and S Quadrant Member is immersing himself in the intricacies of his business entity, and B Quadrant Member is going over papers in his corner office, I Quadrant Member is playing golf with other I Quadrant Members.

How an understanding of the Quadrants Play into MLM A profound understanding of the ESBI Quadrant is a determinant in whether or not an MLM player will find success or failure in his/her future. When you find yourself with personality traits that bear resemblances to those who are in the E and S Quadrants, then it is highly likely you will not find success in MLM. However, if you find yourself possessing personality traits with those on the B and I Quadrants, then your chances of succeeding increase a hundredfold (more or less). It's all about analyzing parallels and consistencies between you and the characteristics of the people who were assigned to various quadrants. When you are able to identify yourself to a certain quadrant, you can further analyze your situation in a more systemic manner. This perspective enables you to map out possible adjustments that you need to be making to put yourself in positions to succeed.

Why Being in the E or S Quadrants Spell Failure

Let's take a look at the personality traits, methodologies, and overall outlooks of those who belong to the E and S Quadrants. They are unwilling to place themselves in risky or compromising situations. They are reluctant to entertain any challenges of growth and development. They don't try to look at the bigger picture, and they don't have a good understanding of financial statements and data. They are overly self-reliant and self-dependent to a fault. They place loads of pressure on themselves, and they can turn to no one else to help them. These traits are undoubtedly character qualities that you will find in people who are the most likely to fail at MLM.

2. Non - Coachable

The most successful people are always those who are comfortable with being the dumbest person in the room. The people who fail are always hard-headed, close-minded, and reluctant to be taught new things or given new perspectives. MLM players who don't know how to accept criticism or advice are those who are likely to fail; and fail hard. The best kind of people in the world are those who are able to recognize people who are better than them; people who they can learn from.

In an MLM scheme, recognizing talent is tantamount to finding success. If you are able to accurately pinpoint people have shown to be knowledgeable in their craft, and if you are open-minded enough to actually learn from these people, then that is always a good sign. The constant losers in the MLM scheme are those who are uncomfortable with stepping outside of their personal perspectives. They are the ones who don't heed advice from those in authority to grant it. There are monumental negative values in one's incapability to be receptive of guided learning and development.

Coaching plays a vital role in the development of an organization and it organically manifests itself best in three particular ways:

i. Systematic Change

A lot of times, organizations will restructure, or revamp policies in efforts to maximize efficiency and productivity.

And even more times, people who are incapable of adapting and/or coping with these changes, will find themselves on the outside looking in very quickly. When radical change occurs within an organization, and parameters are tuned to settings that are unfamiliar to you, that is where coaching comes in very handy. A competent immediate team leader will be able to guide a coachable team mate fairly efficiently to allow them to adapt to such rapid changes in the organization's business processes.

ii.   Performance Improvement

There is no method that is better trusted than that of performance reviews and coaching when it comes to team mate development. When you are lagging behind your work or not living up to the expectations that are set for you, coaching is a great way to get out of that hole. An immediate team leader's role in determining your development as a player is of utmost importance. More often than not, a leader or a coach will always be able to accurately gauge whether or not a team mate is living up to his/her potential.

Uncoachable team mates will never be able to maximize their potential because of their reluctance to develop under the guidance of others.

iii.   Team Building

Team building and growing the team is a task that all of MLM players have embedded deep in their ideological foundations. It's a goal that everyone has at the back of their minds. Most people who are able to accurately realize these goals are those who understand that you need help from those who are already above you in order to progress further. As you climb higher and higher, tasks will get more difficult; responsibilities will become heavier. Most of the time, the gravity of newer situations will overwhelm you, and the uncoachables will always crumble. Those who are eager to learn from those who have already been there will do just fine.

Four Characteristics of Coachable

i. People Humility

This is the foundation of a coachable person. When MLM enthusiasts are able to swallow their pride and acknowledge their own vulnerabilities, then those are the first signs of being gifted with the coachable genes. A humble person knows that there will always be people who are better than them, and that there are things that he/she has yet to learn in order to succeed.

ii. Discipline

Having a willingness to learn, and having the willingness to do the things you need to do to improve are two completely different things. Where humility is a realization of your potential for improvement, discipline is the resolve that is needed to actualize your development and growth as an individual. An undisciplined mind is a stubborn mind, and a stubborn mind will make for slow and ineffective learning.

iii. Curiosity

There's absolutely nothing wrong being curious. Albert Einstein himself attributes his success to his high levels of curiosity. Curiosity is the drive that reinforces your willingness to learn and be taught. Curiosity is where learning and development stems from. Finding a right coach to harness your curiosity and bring forth productive development from it is very important.

iv. Competent Cognitive Ability

This is the final and probably the most important characteristic of a coachable person. One always needs to attain a satisfactory level of cognitive ability in order to be coachable. There is absolutely no use for humility, discipline, and curiosity when one is virtually incapable of developing a grasp of difficult ideas. This manifests itself in situations like when someone cannot understand the principles, an income statement, or financial projections.

3. Self-Development

While coaching is indeed an important aspect in the development of an MLM enthusiast, there is only so much a coach can do to help turn you into a winner. The most successful people are always going to be humble enough to acknowledge that they didn't get to where they are without the help of others, but they are also confident enough to know that a large part of their success was because of their inner being. A person's drive to excel is difficult to put down, and one's zeal for self-development is always important in determining whether or not a person succeeds. Finding innovative ways to constantly develop as a person and as a corporate player is absolutely essential to achieving your personal goals and aspirations. Simple acts like reading up on books of related fields or engaging in deep reflections and analyses on how you conduct your work are all contributors to self-development.

You don't necessarily need to be alone in your struggles for yourself, but there's nothing wrong with developing a sense of independence. Employee Mindset "I'm doing fine for now. I'm comfortable where I am." That's the employee mindset. Going back to Kiyosaki's ESBI Quadrants, the lowest quadrant is the employee quadrant, and it's the lowest quadrant for a good reason. A quadrant that hosts a school of people who are not ambitious, who are not driven, and who lack a zeal for success. These are people who are perfectly fine with being comfortable, and who are always oblivious to the bigger picture. These are people who don't want any part of the bigger scheme of things, and that is why they are unlikely to ever find mass success in their lives. "That is not my job!" This is another phrase that you commonly hear from those with the employee mindset. They are always very particular with the amount of work that they are required to do and the responsibilities that are granted upon them.

A successful person will always understand that whatever role he/she plays in an organization is extremely vital in determining the eventual future of that organization. A successful person will do things that he/she isn't required to do because he/she understands that it is essential to the overall dynamic of the organization structure. The successful people are not bound by their job descriptions, and are always looking to find ways to develop themselves and the organizations that they are a part of. "I'm not comfortable with responsibility." This is perhaps the most damning quality of all for those who are cursed with the employee mindset. They don't understand that working towards success is also equivalent to a gradual progression of one's responsibilities.

Unsuccessful people will most likely turn down opportunities for success because they give in to their fears of failure and responsibility. The successful people will always take on these risks and carry the burdens of responsibility in order to place themselves in positions for success. One of the most common reasons for MLM people who get behind is because of their reluctance to assume greater responsibilities for the work that they do.

4. Money Driven

When you get into the MLM game, what exactly are you doing it for? Is it for practical purposes? Are there personal goals that you have to accomplish in order to preserve your integrity as an individual? Are you merely bored with your life, and are looking for something productive to do with your spare time? Whatever your reason is, it's always best to know it by heart. Motivation plays a huge role in just about any undertaking we choose to engage in as a species.

Motivation is what gets us out of bed every morning to live our individual lives. Motivation dictates the quality of life that we want for ourselves and for those around us. So it shouldn't come as a surprise that motivation also plays an incredibly vital role in determining your success as an MLM player. Yes. We all want to be rich and amass enough money to live comfortable and stable lives. We all want to be placed in positions of financial security.

However, don't forget, that's the same kind of mentality that eventually led to the downfall of Bruno in the Parable of the Pipeline.

Yes, money can be a very good motivator at the start of any career path. There's nothing like experiencing the fruits of your labor, and going out and spending your first pay check on something fancy. The problem with money being your motivation in your business dealings is that it doesn't usually bode well in the long-term.

Let's go back to the Parable of the Pipeline. Bruno was motivated by wealth, and the luxuries that money could afford. His motivations led him to small-minded thinking that didn't benefit him the bigger scheme of things. Pablo recognized the value of money, but he understood that instant money shouldn't be his biggest motivator. He was motivated on a daily basis by the possibility of a dream coming true. His dream of having a water pipeline that would sustain him for the rest of his life was what made him get out of bed every morning and work endlessly until success came to him.

Now, that isn't to say your motivation should be to build a pipeline. The point here is that there are ideas out there that can serve as better motivations for productivity than money. In reality, you can motivate yourself with the possibility of fulfilling your goals for innovation; motivate yourself by working hard to ensure the stability of the organization that you're a part of; or you could motivate yourself to provide a better life for those you care about.

At the end of the day, while money is important, it is not the only part of the picture.

5. Poor Time Management

This is absolutely a no-brainer. The world of MLM is very competitive and highly unforgiving. There are loads and loads of other players who are striving to get ahead of each other, and time is indeed of the essence.

Remember the Parable of the Pipeline with Pablo and Bruno? Time management played a huge role in that story. They were both granted the same amount of time every day, 24 hours. Of course, no one can work for 24 hours straight, 7 days a week. That is unhealthy and downright counterproductive. So out of the 24 hours that you get every day to do your work, make sure that you divide your time efficiently that produces the most gains. However, it's again important to stress that the gains need not necessarily be immediate. Bruno was so engrossed in immediate rewards, and he dedicated all of his working time into getting instant gratification. Pablo was wiser and more efficient with how he handled his time. He worked just enough daily to help him scrape by on a day-to-day basis, but he also allotted time for accomplishing his long-term goals that ended up benefitting him in the long run. This concept is called Embracing the Grind.

Sure, plotting out your schedule for productivity and developing a routine on a daily basis may seem very mundane; but this method is what gets the most amount of work done in the most efficient manner. It's not a new discovery. This method has been tried, tested, and trusted by successful people over the course of history. Modern human civilization was and is continually being built by people who understand the principles of time management and the role it plays in productivity.

Poor time management leads to burn outs and lower productivity when an MLM practitioner fails to manage his/her time efficiently in a manner that boosts productivity, then that's a recipe for disaster. Anyone who can't seem to properly divide their time in accomplishing their tasks will always end up feeling overworked and unaccomplished. You'd be surprised to find out that people who are able to manage their time efficiently actually get more work done without feeling stressed or worn down.

These are simple principles of success that aren't so obvious to many people, not especially to those who are prone to failure. As the cliché goes, time is gold. You are sitting on a goldmine of time every single day of your life, and it would be a shame if you didn't manage it properly.

When it comes to time management while working in a multi level marketing company, the line between work and family time can get a bit blurred. A dedicated sales person can easily find themselves caught in a perpetual spiral of chaos, jumping from an event to a meeting to a family dinner, and back to a client's home. We can gain an income, but lose some of the real life satisfaction if we don't maintain a grip on time management. Dedication doesn't mean we have to forget about our life, and our families. A time management plan is a good thing to include with our networking marketing plan.

Yes, we plan to sell, and sell a lot, BUT, we also have a family. Balance is a necessary part of life, and so are realistic goals.

Here are 7 things that aid in time management.

i. Create a daily power hour.

During that time you can connect with perspective clients, build relationships with clients, follow up on potential client calls, read or work on self development, or even have a short webinar or training session with team members.

ii. Make a to do list for work.

We often think we can do more, or less, than we are capable of. If we utilize a to do list, we will learn our own limitations and eventually create the perfect upkeep list. We have to tone down on some activities, watch our time limits more carefully and not get overwhelmed with how long the list seems. Whatever we do, it can only be done one thing at a time, with the exception of social media thanks to programs like Hadoop.

iii. Make an achievements list.

Every week, take the time to write down the achievements you have accomplished during the week. T the end of the month, take the time to look over the things you have successfully finished and give yourself a pat on the back. It doesn't all have to be about work.

iv. The four D's, delete, delegate defer and diminish.

Take the time to ponder your to do list and evaluate what takes dominion. Utilize the four D's to create realistic to do lists by delegating responsibility to others when possible, deferring things to a later time when reasonable, diminish unnecessary tasks, and delete things that are irrelevant or unreliable.

v. Walk away and take a break sometimes.

It is important to take breaks and walk away sometimes. We all need to take time to breath.

vi. Make a work schedule.

Look at when you usually meet with clients, and your peak digital media times. Evaluate what your most profitable time frames are and make yourself a schedule. We have to have time to live and enjoy the lifestyle our hard work is paying for.

vii. Use all available technology.

Such as eCommerce, social media, digital technology and mobile applications. This is a real time saver on all accounts and can really open the door to quick, easy sales. So why do people fail? Realistically, in most cases people fail because they choose too. We have choices in life and some may seem a bit uncertain. However, if we trust in ourselves and our own capabilities, set realistic goals, and achieve them, we can succeed in the MLM industry with flying colours. If you lack motivation and inspiration, and require a time clock, with someone telling you what to do in life, this might not be the business for you.

Notes

9. "Pipeline" Pablo and Bruno Story

In this chapter, we invoke some principles that were laid out in a bestselling book called The Parable of the Pipeline by Burke Hedges. The book begins with a simple short story depicting the adventures of two central characters, Pablo and Bruno. This story's lessons have been used by prominent academics, financial advisers, life coaches, and more because of its simple premise and profound insights on finding financial security.

The story's summary is as follows:

A Summary of the Parable "In a small village near a beautiful valley, there resided two friends, Pablo and Bruno. They were both young, ambitious, and hardworking fellows. They often spent their days discussing their personal dreams and aspirations with each other. They wanted to become the most successful men in the village. They were constantly in search of opportunities to succeed. One day, the mayor of the village announced that he would pay a decent amount of money to two people for a simple task: gather fresh water that could be found in a spring on top of the mountain and deliver it across the valley, back into the village. They each would be paid based on the amount of water that they could retrieve.

Bruno and Pablo volunteered immediately with much enthusiasm.

To start, Bruno and Pablo were incredibly hardworking, and they had much rewards to show for their efforts. They were delivering water from the mountain into the village in rapid paces with multiple roundtrips bearing a bucket in each hand. Bruno was satisfied with his pace of income and with his work output. He thought to himself to use bigger buckets in delivering water so as to increase his productivity and eventual wages. He incentivized himself with the prospects of using his wages to buy a bigger house and a cow.

Pablo however, took a different approach and thought of an idea. He wanted to build a pipeline that connected the mountain spring directly into the village. He brought his idea to Bruno and Bruno laughed at his face commenting that it would take too much time and too much work to build a pipeline

So they set about their separate paths as workers.

Bruno ended up being more productive than Pablo on the offset, because Pablo spent most of his time building a pipeline and minimal time using the bucket delivery system. They carried on like this for more than two years. In that two year span, Bruno had amassed a great amount of wealth, a bigger house, a cow, and a leisurely lifestyle. However, he had grown tired and worn from the amount of work he was doing, and this was work that he still needed to do on a daily basis to maintain his lifestyle.

After two years of toiling, Pablo finally finished his pipeline and water flowed effortlessly into the village. Pablo was earning more money than ever before. He was now watching his earnings grow rapidly without having to shed a single drop of sweat."

Lessons from the Parable The Parable of the Pipeline symbolize the two basic means to go about finding financial security in life. There are people like Bruno who are absolute work horses and they carry buckets back and forth in order to amass their wages.

To increase their income, people like Bruno had to either increase the size of their buckets or increase the amount of trips that they made to the water source. Increasing the amount of trips to the water source can be likened to working multiple jobs or working overtime shifts to increase income. Increasing the size of the bucket is similar to getting higher paying jobs that amount to more difficult and strenuous work. People like Bruno are willing to trade in their time for money. What they don't account for is when they get to a situation wherein time will rob them of their opportunities, and they will not be able to sustain themselves with the time that is allotted to them.

Robbed time can be attributed to old age, sickness, and other such factors. In contrast to Bruno's method, Pablo used his time in a different manner. He allotted only a minimal amount of his time to work that granted him immediate income, and used the rest of his time for building the pipeline. He knew that while the pipeline would not grant him instant reward, once completed, it would increase his potential for earning more income by a great deal. The best part of Pablo's pipeline plan is that it was immune to personal vulnerabilities on his part because it could survive on its own with minimal oversight.

6. How Does the Parable Relate to MLM?

It's fairly simple. The MLM practitioners who have a Bruno-mentality in how they go about business are highly likely to fail. Why so? Bruno only found value in the small pictures and the instant successes he had had. He didn't have a long-term view on his financial situation and his capacities as a laborer. He did not prepare any contingencies for unforeseen conditions and he was not forward thinking. He was deeply engrossed in the prospects of immediate rewards, he ended up failing to analyze the sustainability of his methods. Competitors in the MLM game should be wary of falling into the traps of comfort and stagnancy. While there is no insatiable need to really reinvent the wheel per se, there is always value in innovation and in doing things that aren't being done by everyone else (granted that they're effective in their methods). When MLM players succumb to the leisure of routine and consistency, that may just end up spelling doom for them in the long run.

Credits for photos of Pablo and Bruno pipeline are screenshots from

https://www.youtube.com/watch?v=sSKxvJdYOu8

Notes

10. 7 Proven Strategies to Building a Network Marketing Empire in 12 months

It would be considered a major understatement to say that building a marketing empire is a difficult task to undertake. There are numerous factors that go into creating a successful business empire; factors like skill, proper networking, time management, hard work, and some healthy doses of good luck. That being said, it may come out as an oversimplification of the discipline to say that there exists a blueprint that is designed to help people find success in this industry. So yes, while this chapter seeks to establish itself as a blueprint for success, do not, under any circumstances, believe that building a massive marketing empire is a matter of ticking items of a checklist. While chapters and insights like this do claim to offer a framework for success, your achievements still heavily depend on your own volition and convictions as an MLM practitioner.

1. Choosing the right leader

Here, we are talking about the right leader. Not the richest or smartest or prettiest leader.

Almost ALL of the leading companies have one thing in common. They are run by great leaders. Any company cannot grow from a small startup to a big company without good leadership.

Here are some of the characteristics to look for in a good leader.

A leader appreciates his/her people.

People love to be praised if they've done something great. The praises should come from the team head. When you are a leader, you need to observe the activities of your team members and single out those who are doing excellent stuff.

It may seem insignificant, but it is a superb way of boosting their self-esteem, making them perform better.

Leaders are available

What is the use of heads if they aren't available? It is utterly foolish for a leader to claim that he/she runs a team when he/she can't be reached by phone, e-mail or text. Team members might need to consult over an issue, so you need to be reachable. When the communication flows freely, then they can count on a leader who is available.

Leaders stay calm when facing diversity

Fear and weakness is part of every human being. At some point, the vision might seem unclear, but the leader must always be sure about the MLM training system and the business itself. The team members may also feel hopeless, and the only hope they have is their leader. Whenever they realize that the leader is also unsure, just like them, they'll look for someone else to lead them.

Good leaders usually go to the company whenever they face any problems. When the company executives know what's happening, they'll try to fix it. A good leader goes back to his people and tells them everything is going to be alright.

Links the corporate staff to their team

Good leaders desire to connect the company's staff to their team members. These people might be working in different locations, but in the real sense, they're working towards a common goal. They are trying to sell the same brand of products. When the creator of a product meets the distributor, there develops a sense of belonging. The distributors meet the one man who defines their career path, and the creator meets people passionate about getting his product to the masses. The result is the company develops, all thanks to the visionary leader.

Leaders should be morally upright

A leader should naturally be a role model. The team members are ready to follow orders when they know they are taking them from a person who cares about ethics. When the leader is so keen on using shortcuts to get what they want, they lose the belief of their team members.

A leader should also know that everyone has goals. The team members are always growing, and this happens at different levels. Some may bring many clients to a session, some a few and others none. It's not the time to start criticizing but rather commend those who have improved and those who are still looking.

Training sessions are also vital for MLM, and great leaders are the ones to organize them. The product developer should be part of these meetings. He/she doesn't need to attend the meeting physically. The leader may arrange for a conference, audio or video call if it is clear that the specialist will not be present physically. The action might seem meaningless, but it will reinforce the belief the team has on the product/service. When you have applied these strategies, there's no doubt about your success in MLM.

2. **Chase the Right People and Avoid Chasing Family and Friends**

The whole idea of Network Marketing revolves around the premise of building a corporate mechanism that is so strong, that it is able to function as a self-sustaining entity. It is important to note that this corporate mechanism is only going to be as strong as the people that it is composed of. In order to build a respectable Network Marketing Empire, it is absolutely essential that you find the right people to surround yourself with. Previous chapters have already discussed the importance characteristics and traits that are found within successful people. Take advantage of this knowledge and gather a team of skilled professionals who are ready to serve as the building blocks for your marketing empire. A lot of times, choosing the wrong people will do more harm than anyone can expect. It only takes one wrong person at the wrong place and wrong time to make an entire corporate kingdom fall and crumble to its knees.

So while finding the right people to help you build your empire might seem like a daunting and exhaustive task, it doesn't have to be. Getting to interact with others is a great way to develop as a leader and as a person. Gathering perspective and being open-minded to alternative views is most ideal for someone who is looking to build a business empire. You should always approach people-finding as a great way to expand your network, and proper tool to gauge the kind of talent that you want to surround yourself with. More often than not, you will run into people who have nothing positive to offer, but don't consider these meetings to be a waste of your time. Reflect on these kinds of people, and analyze trending personality traits that you like about them, and use this information as a way to solidify the identity of your corporate kingdom.

A lot of people don't understand that even a business entity can have a personality, and even fewer people understand that the business entities with the most appealing personalities are those that always find success. Find out now the kind of personality of the kind of marketing empire that you want to be building, and use this as a rubric in your people-finding and recruitment missions.

While it may be easy to chase after family and friends to hit your recruitment numbers, it's not always best idea. First off, your family and friends might not necessarily make for great resources in building a massive network marketing empire. Next, it would make for a very awkward situation to have work lives mixing with personal lives. Lastly, the best talent can be found outside your circle of acquaintances, and you don't ever want to box yourself in with only the people you know.

To further elaborate on the point of structures taking the shape of personalities, it's also very important that you recognize the value of humanity in network marketing empires. It is the people who will help you build this money-making mechanism that you envision in your head, and it is the people who you should always prioritize. It's always best to remember that the people you work with are exactly that – people. They have feelings, they have dreams, aspirations, goals, and visions, the same way that you do. These are all facets of their being that make up their entire personality. The key in building a well-functioning network marketing empire is in harnessing the energy of these personalities into something that is united and productive.

Always make an effort to get to know the people you work with and build actual working relationships with them that transcend traditional job descriptions. Find out their motivations and analyze how you can use their motivations as tools to boost productivity and effectiveness. Finding the right people to fit particular jobs can be very difficult, but when you do get over that initial struggle, everything else comes easy. The right people will know and understand your needs as an MLM Player, and they also realize their roles in shaping the corporate entity as a whole. You will not be able to find and keep the right people if you do not allow yourself to build a relationship with them that goes beyond face-value.

3. The Sales-Recruitment Dynamic

As the head of a massive network marketing empire, it's your job to keep your eyes on the bigger picture. Yes. Attention-to-detail is very important in whatever we do in life, but we must be wary to not get lost in the nitty-gritties, that we end up losing sight of the bigger picture. Sales are very important. Sales enable a business's income flow, and this income is used to either keep the company afloat, or to expand. Sales are the basic lifeblood of a business structure, and it is pointless to keep a business venture going when sales aren't enough. That is a very important idea that no one in their right minds would ever question. However, unsuccessful people fall for this trap far too often: They think that businesses start and end with sales.

There is a bigger picture out there, and that picture is that of a robot-like business mechanism that brings in income with minimal effort and oversight. That mechanism however, is not built by sales, it is built by people – people who you recruit. As important as it is to have a strong and stable sales system in place, it is just as important to have a solid recruitment system in place, particularly in network marketing – where people make for the best resources.

There are various recruitment tools that take advantage of technology and software out in the market today. The better-developed recruitment systems actually enable for targeted recruitment for your company. These systems help you pick the right people that will fit right into the vision that you have for your network marketing empire. It might be important to consider these as options for recruitment methodologies, but this is only one option. The point of this entire segment is to not overlook the importance of recruitment. If you're going to be investing so much of your business's resources in stable sales systems, it would be wise to be investing just as much into your recruitment systems.

Part of having a team of skilled professionals who you can trust and rely on is being able to afford the luxuries of delegation. As the head of a massive network marketing empire, it's important that you keep yourself afloat amidst the sea of little details that you have to pay attention to every single day. You also have the major responsibility of setting the direction of your business empire, and constantly be in the lookout for major trends in the marketing world that you can use to redefine or revamp your entity's business processes.

All of this work can be incredibly overwhelming, and you have to remember the bigger picture that we've been constantly talking about. The goal is for you to build a mechanism that is so sound and solid, that you only need to perform minimal oversight. That's what having a right time of people can give you. You have to learn to delegate tasks and responsibilities to the people you work with. The reason why you go through very strenuous recruitment processes is because you want to be assured that you are getting the right people. Now is the time to reap the fruits of your labor by having your team work for you. The level of empowerment that you grant to the people you work with can make or break your entire business structure. Granting people with bigger roles and responsibilities affirms their value to the team and to the empire that you're building.

4. New Age Marketing

If there's one phenomenal marvel that has shaped society in a most significant manner in the new millennium, it is the phenomenon of social media. Social Media has somehow found a way to bridge gaps in data and information like no other tool has been able to in the past. News, relationships, business transactions, political dealings, and cultural transformations are heavily influenced by social media in this new age. Only fools would disregard social media's role in the new age of network marketing, and you can't afford to be a fool in building your kingdom.

Social Media Marketing can be a daunting tool for those who are set in traditional patterns of network marketing, but that is why only the adaptable and coachable can survive. In order for you to build a well-functioning marketing empire, you need to be able to maximize this tool to further your gains and potential.

Millions and millions of dollars are being exchanged on social media sites every month. All sorts of companies, whether big or small, have enabled transaction mechanisms on social media accounts to further boost their sales outputs. Recruitment firms are utilizing social media as a means to acquire the best talent for employers. With the limitless number of tools that social media can provide to your company, it would be foolish to let any of them go to waste.

You can use Facebook, Twitter, YouTube, or Instagram accounts to advertise your business's products or your recruitment openings. You can use social media sites as a resource for data and trends within the MLM community. You can direct your recruits to various target markets with the use of simple search queries on social media sites. Being social media savvy is absolutely imperative when you're looking to build a network marketing empire that puts all others to shame.

A much underused, but very effective method to boost product sales for MLM empires is to tap social media bloggers and socialites to review your products. The reason why this method is very effective is because bloggers tend to project a third-party and impartial view when marketing your products to prospective buyers. It's as simple as sending over some of your business empire's products over to prominent bloggers, social media celebrities, and socialites to review on their personal websites, Instagram accounts, or Facebook pages. This is new-age advertising that has proven to be effective time and time over, and you can't afford not to make use of his method of marketing.

Bloggers and social media celebrities will also boost online traffic for your products when it comes to search engine queries. When they blog about your products, or post about your business on their websites, that means more internet exposure for you on social media sites and on search engine results. The most popular bloggers will have a solid fan base who will be susceptible to their endorsements and you must take advantage of this fact.

Don't forget that sales are the lifeblood of your business and income flow is what's going to keep your marketing empire afloat, and the best way to generate sales is with innovative marketing. Target bloggers or social media celebrities who appeal mostly to the demographics of your target market. It wouldn't make sense to spend money on international celebrity endorses to market your products when they won't even appeal to the people in your target market. Social media celebrities and bloggers offer a more personal and reachable approach to marketing, and that always spells success for companies who now how to make the most of it.

Gaining access to the data that search engines can provide you is easier now than it has ever been. You can use the information and data that you collect from search engine results to shape your marketing, sales, and recruitment campaigns. Find out which of your products have maximum internet coverage, and adjust your marketing schemes accordingly. Understand marketing trends that are going on in the MLM community, and make sure to stay ahead of the curve. If people want to know more about anything these days, a Google search is their most likely approach. Take advantage of this fact and make sure you have a solid online presence. Make use of Search Engine Optimization (SEO) techniques to make sure that your business and products are ranked high on the landing pages.

Search Engines can serve as valuable resources for expanding the reach of your products and when you are able to tap into these resources, you are putting yourself in a position to succeed. Expand your visibility on the internet, and you're also bound to expand the reach of your network marketing empire as well.

5. Learn to Follow-Up

In the complicated field of recruitment, independent studies have shown that initial meetings are likely to not have profound effects on potential recruits or clients. When you first introduce the mechanics of your corporate structure or your business's products to someone, it's difficult to convey that information into terms that resonate with them personally. Factors like language, demeanor, charisma, and setting all play vital roles during initial meet-ups but they can only do so much. Hence, the need for follow-ups.

It's very rare to come across someone who will join your team upon first exposure to your business model. The art of follow-ups are absolutely necessary in building your competent and reliable work force. The best way to go about your recruitment process is to pattern it in a way that is organic and not overwhelming. Use every meet-up as an opportunity to introduce something new and interesting about the business entity that you are a part of. Don't bombard them with all of your big guns in just one meeting. Give them enough information that will get them interested, but also leave out some details that will entice them to want to meet up with you again.

Remember to be persistent, but not annoying in your follow-up efforts. You want to be able to walk that line very deliberately and strike a balance between being determined and irritating. You can also use third-party endorsements from trusted individuals to help strengthen your case during follow-up sessions. This is where endorsements from bloggers, social media celebrities, or perhaps close friends of potential recruits will come in. This will help solidify your stature as a legitimate business entity.

Never forget that it takes a substantial amount of patience to build your network marketing empire, and while the follow-up methodology of recruitment may seem overly strenuous, it has proven to be effective. Just stick with the grind and make sure that you stay motivated with the prospect of chasing the right people to help you build your kingdom.

More often than not, people fall victim to being a jack of all trades, but a master of none. It's the same situation in the scheme of network marketing. When you are constantly trying to be an innovative player in the field, it's always best to develop yourself in a certain niche. Yes, it pays to be well-rounded, but it pays even more to be known as a master at particular aspects of business.

There is a learning curve for absolutely everyone and you are no exemption to the rule. We can only be as brilliant as our cognitive abilities can allow us to be, and once we realize this, the easier it is to understand why it's better to stick to one or two methodologies at a given time. If you're skilled at face-to-face marketing and recruitment, then work on that skill until you are unrivaled in that area. Don't bother venturing into other areas of marketing like analytics or data-driven recruitment if you're not yet familiar with those methodologies. It's always best to work with the tools that are available to you. These are the proper recipes for finding success in recruitment. When your strengths are absolutely flawless and have reached their ceiling, perhaps then it is time to branch out and try new things.

6. Duplication

One of the ways you can be successful in network marketing is by learning how to duplicate. Most of the people who do not make it in MLM usually care less about duplication. What most people have in mind when starting out is that they have to get thousands of people to join to ensure they are successful. Such a mentality will never get your team members anywhere. What you need to do is get at least two individuals who are hungry for success. Convince them to look for two more people – and the list will continue to grow. Two to four to eight to sixteen to thirty-two to sixty-four to one hundred and twenty-eight to … Power of duplication.

When you don't tell your team members this during the training sessions, it will be difficult for the duplication process to work. It is a strategy that works and can be replicated by your team members. You must also ensure that all your team members can use the strategies for duplication.

To build something big out of network marketing, you need to work with people. What you should concentrate on is how many people duplicate you. The idea is simple: sponsoring someone who then sponsors someone else who sponsors the other. That's how it's supposed to work. Sharing your brand of products with prospective distributors is good. They get to see them and also see the benefits. These are people who in most cases want to make some extra cash.

You may make some money retailing the products but what's even better is sponsoring new distributors. It is a challenge for most new distributors. They compare themselves to people who have been in the game for some time and some might even visualize themselves failing. At this point, it will be up to the team leader to train them and give them motivation.

The training , some call the New Members/Distributors Orientation Training should happen in the first month when new , where the new distributors get to apply what they are learning.

When you have gotten your team members to do duplication, you will start reaping the fruits. Once you are in the MLM business, endurance is all you need to keep you above others doing the same business.

When you manage to sponsor a small number of distributors, your task will now be to get them to train and sponsor others just like you did.

When you fail to train them to do that, it will be difficult for them to stay motivated and that means you will lose leads. Sharing the products with people is also vital because they will experience them and see their benefits once they become distributor. Retailing should then be taken seriously because they connect you with prospective distributors.

7. Your "Why"

This is the most fundamental key in building your empire; the empire that you have envisioned for yourself and those who are with you on this journey. It's always imperative for you to never forget your "why". When you are constantly reinforcing your own motivations upon yourself, you also end up building your personal character and the character of the empire that you are building. When you don't lose sight of your motivations, the people who work with you won't forget their motivations either. Motivations are what drive us to get out of bed every morning and contribute something productive to the world. When you stay motivated, you are driven to demand excellence from yourself and those you work with. When the people around you stay motivated, they are driven to perform to the highest of standards, and to deliver quality results. It is okay to become entrenched with the other questions that plague our daily lives.

"Who do I have to meet today for my sales pitch?"

"What are the numbers from last month's recruitment campaign?"

"When are we going to hit our quarterly goals?"

"Where do we have to go to branch out our company's production reach?"

Questions like these are all very important in shaping our day-to-day productivity, but in the bigger scheme of things, there is no bigger question than: "Why do I still do what I do?"

Building a self-sustaining corporate entity is no easy task, but it doesn't have to be so difficult. What this chapter seeks to highlight are merely common trends that are present in the narratives of successful business structures, and how you can use these trends to increase your chances of finding success. These are tried, tested, and trusted methodologies that have helped successful people in the realization of their corporate goals. Just read, study, and learn these valuable principles to place yourself in the most ideal position to succeed. Whatever comes next is up to you.

Notes

ABOUT THE AUTHOR

Mervyn Chan is regarded by many as a young superstar expert all over the world in Network Marketing. He is well known to be fast as he created 5 figures passive income stream in just less than 8 weeks. Rather than "rah-rah" type Mervyn focuses on specific, how to training and coaching to build the business faster.

With many trial and errors from different companies and structures, he ultimately discovered a proven working system.

Within a short span of 8 weeks, not only did he generated a 5 figure passive income stream, his organization grabbed foothold in Colombia, Panama, Costa Rica, Chile, Peru, Brunei, Malaysia and of course his hometown, Singapore.

Got a feedback? Looking for partnership? Want a consultation or coaching?

Contact Mervyn Chan at
+65 9727 2958 or email him at
ask@MervynChan.com

Made in the USA
Lexington, KY
18 December 2016